A History

~ of ~

Nova Scotia

~ in ~

50 Objects

NIMBUS
PUBLISHING
nimbus.ca

Joan Dawson

Nimbus Publishing Limited
3731 Mackintosh St, Halifax, NS B3K 5A5
(902) 455-4286 nimbus.ca

Printed and bound in Canada

NB1125
Design: Peggy & Co. Design

The quotation from Marjorie Whitelaw's book, *First Impressions*, is used with the kind
permission of the Nova Scotia Museum.

Library and Archives Canada Cataloguing in Publication

Dawson, Joan, 1932-, author
A history of Nova Scotia in 50 objects / Joan Dawson.

Includes bibliographical references.
Issued in print and electronic formats.
ISBN 978-1-77108-295-2 (pbk.).—ISBN 978-1-77108-296-9 (html)

1. Nova Scotia—History. 2. Material culture—Nova Scotia. I. Title.

FC2319.D39 2015   971.6   C2015-900249-4
C2015-900250-8

Canada Council Conseil des arts
for the Arts   du Canada

FILM & CREATIVE INDUSTRIES

Nimbus Publishing acknowledges the financial support for its publishing activities from the
Government of Canada through the Canada Book Fund (CBF) and the Canada Council for the
Arts, and from the Province of Nova Scotia through Film & Creative Industries Nova Scotia. We
are pleased to work in partnership with Film & Creative Industries Nova Scotia to develop and
promote our creative industries for the benefit of all Nova Scotians.

*This book is dedicated
to the volunteers, past and present,
at Fort Point Museum, LaHave.*

Contents

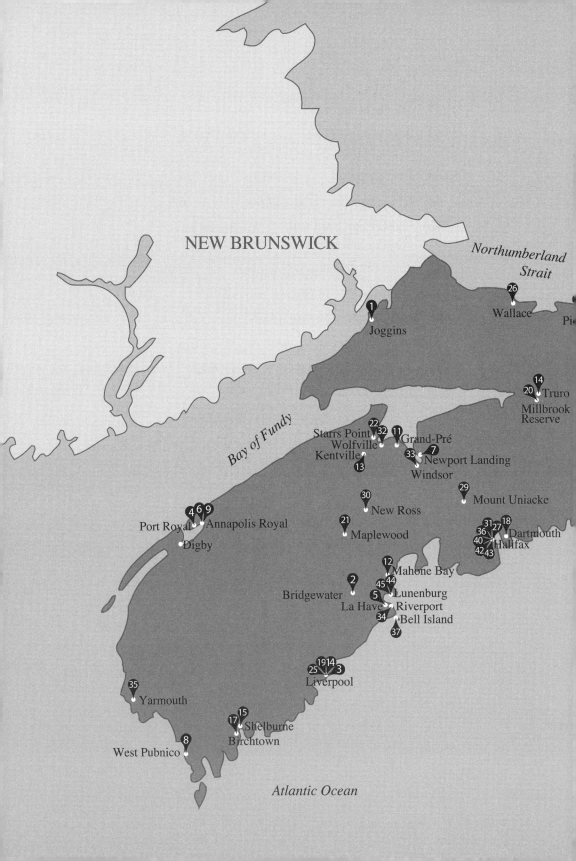

NEW BRUNSWICK

Northumberland Strait

26
Wallace

Pi

1
Joggins

14
20 Truro
Millbrook
Reserve

Bay of Fundy

22
32 11
Starrs Point   Grand-Pré
Wolfville   33
Kentville   Newport Landing
13   Windsor   7

29
30   Mount Uniacke
New Ross

4 6 9   21   31 18
Port Royal   Annapolis Royal   Maplewood   36 27 Dartmouth
Digby   40   Halifax
42 43

12
Mahone Bay
2   45 44
Bridgewater   5   Lunenburg
La Have   Riverport
34   Bell Island
37

19 14
25   3
Liverpool

35
Yarmouth

15
17   Shelburne
Birchtown

8
West Pubnico

Atlantic Ocean

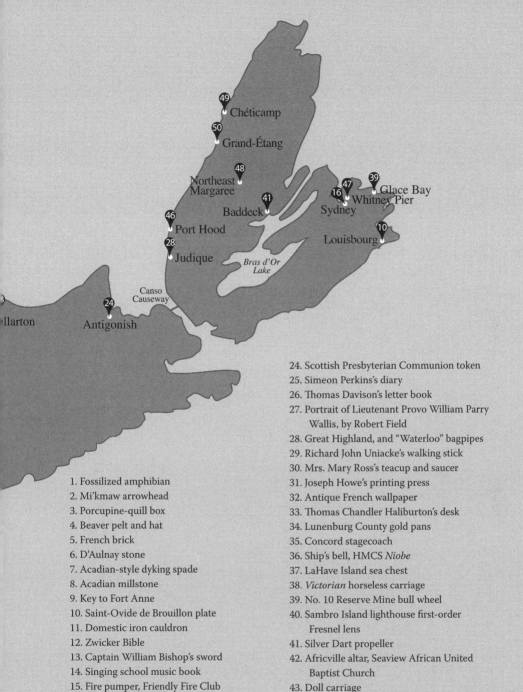

Chéticamp 49
Grand-Étang 50
Northeast Margaree 48
Baddeck 41
Port Hood 46
Judique 28
Whitney Pier 47
Glace Bay 39
Sydney 16
Louisbourg 10
Bras d'Or Lake
Canso Causeway
Antigonish 24
llarton

1. Fossilized amphibian
2. Mi'kmaw arrowhead
3. Porcupine-quill box
4. Beaver pelt and hat
5. French brick
6. D'Aulnay stone
7. Acadian-style dyking spade
8. Acadian millstone
9. Key to Fort Anne
10. Saint-Ovide de Brouillon plate
11. Domestic iron cauldron
12. Zwicker Bible
13. Captain William Bishop's sword
14. Singing school music book
15. Fire pumper, Friendly Fire Club
16. Loyalist candle mould
17. Black Loyalist pearlware dish
18. Quaker House shoes
19. Whale's tooth with scrimshaw decoration
20. Mi'kmaw woman's cap
21. German butter churn
22. Davenport dessert plate
23. Gentleman's top hat

24. Scottish Presbyterian Communion token
25. Simeon Perkins's diary
26. Thomas Davison's letter book
27. Portrait of Lieutenant Provo William Parry
    Wallis, by Robert Field
28. Great Highland, and "Waterloo" bagpipes
29. Richard John Uniacke's walking stick
30. Mrs. Mary Ross's teacup and saucer
31. Joseph Howe's printing press
32. Antique French wallpaper
33. Thomas Chandler Haliburton's desk
34. Lunenburg County gold pans
35. Concord stagecoach
36. Ship's bell, HMCS *Niobe*
37. LaHave Island sea chest
38. *Victorian* horseless carriage
39. No. 10 Reserve Mine bull wheel
40. Sambro Island lighthouse first-order
    Fresnel lens
41. Silver Dart propeller
42. Africville altar, Seaview African United
    Baptist Church
43. Doll carriage
44. Schooner *Theresa E. Connor*
45. Halifax and South Western Railway
    conductor's hat
46. Angus L. Macdonald's trowel
47. Whitney Pier mailbox
48. Coldstream fly-tying bench
49. Acadian hooked tapestry
50. Seven-headed beast Mi-Carême mask

Preface

I HAVE SPENT MUCH OF THE PAST TWO YEARS HUNTING FOR hidden treasure. No, I was not digging for pirate gold or diving in search of shipwrecks. I was not expecting to make my fortune, but looking for items in Nova Scotia's museums that represent people, places, or events that tell some of the province's most fascinating stories.

I've discovered that treasures can be found in unlikely places. Who would expect to find a British-made eighteenth-century fire engine in a South Shore museum? Or a wedding gift from Edward, Duke of Kent, in the Annapolis Valley? Or the trowel that had laid the cornerstone of a Digby school in a small town in Cape Breton? These and many other interesting surprises awaited me as I journeyed through the province. I visited a variety of museums in Nova Scotia, from federally operated national historic sites, provincial institutions, and heritage houses, to small community museums run by volunteers. I spoke to professional museum staff, dedicated volunteers who helped establish local museums, and student guides funded by government grants. And I met many people from varied communities whose enthusiastic welcome and pride in their museum's artefacts and local history led me to the treasures contained in their collections.

I was inspired to embark on this project after reading Neil MacGregor's fascinating book *The History of the World in 100 Objects*, in which he showed how material items—in his case selected from the vast collection of the British Museum—can tell personal stories or embody the history and culture of a place and an era. I thought of objects I had seen in Nova Scotia's museums that also had interesting connections with people and events of the past. They are not all assembled in one place, like the objects MacGregor describes, but scattered in different locations throughout the province. It is not my intention to write another history book, but to look at Nova Scotia's past through a selection of treasures from its museums, and to hear the stories that they have to tell.

I have selected the objects described in this book for various reasons. Some items cried out to me as I wandered round our wonderful and diverse museums; others were suggested by family and friends, or by curators and guides who led me to their personal favourite objects. I looked for items with tales to tell about people, communities, or significant events. What I found is that Nova Scotia's museums contain so many interesting artefacts, some had to be omitted to keep this book within reasonable limits. And, with regret, I have had to omit some museums altogether, which are no less interesting than those whose treasures I have written about.

I have worked as a volunteer in a community museum, and I know that this can be an enriching experience. It has been equally rewarding to visit other museums, and to see the items in their collections that speak of the generosity of their donors and the dedication of those people, often unpaid and unsung, who have documented their treasures and shared them with me. I am grateful to them all.

—JD

Introduction:
Treasures from Times Past

AT THE TIME OF WRITING, NOVA SCOTIA HAS OVER TWO hundred museums. You may wonder why there are so many in a small province. The Atlantic region has a long history, from its physical formation millions of years ago, through its early aboriginal settlement after the last ice age, to modern times. Its formally recorded history has taken place in the relatively short period of European colonization and development over the past four hundred years. During this time, people from many different backgrounds have come to the province and contributed to its development, and great political, social, and economic changes have taken place. Our museums preserve this history by collecting and displaying items from earlier times that help us to understand the people and events that have shaped the Nova Scotia we know today. These buildings come in all shapes and sizes: Some museums are purpose-built, environmentally controlled establishments. Many more are housed in re-purposed schools, churches, civic buildings, stores, and heritage houses. A few are federally, provincially, or municipally funded, and professionally staffed. Many are operated by volunteers, assisted by government grants but largely dependent on fundraising for their maintenance. Each one reflects some aspect of our history and culture.

For thousands of years before white people came, the Mi'kmaq occupied what is now Nova Scotia, a land whose geological history began billions of years ago. European settlement dates back to the early seventeenth century, when the only parts of what we now call Canada known to the Europeans were the Atlantic coast and the St. Lawrence. The next 150 years saw a protracted struggle between the French and English for control of Nova Scotia. The mid-eighteenth century saw the foundation of Halifax, the Expulsion of the Acadians, and the settlement in Nova Scotia of European Foreign Protestants, who were joined by New England Planters, landless Scots, and post-revolutionary Loyalists, both white and black. All of these settlers made a significant impact on the development of our province. The nineteenth century saw the rapid growth of communities built around the lumbering, shipbuilding, and fishing industries, as well as agricultural development. By its end, change was in the air. The water wheels that drove industry gave way to steam power, wood was replaced by iron for shipbuilding, and sailing vessels were superseded by steamboats. Objects from all of these periods can be found in our museums.

The twentieth century brought still more rapid changes as new technology made traditional practices obsolete and people had to adapt to a different way of life. Industrial development and two world wars brought new immigrants from many European countries and beyond to our shores. During this time, hydroelectric plants replaced sawmills on our rivers, horses and oxen were abandoned for the internal combustion engine, and the pen gave way to typewriters and then to computers. Old machines, tools, and domestic implements that had changed very little over the years suddenly became outdated and were replaced by more efficient machinery and household appliances. The old items were thrown out or relegated to attics, where they gathered dust. But as the century progressed, local heritage and historical societies developed. Their members realized that history was more than a dry series of dates and that objects from the past were worth preserving. Museums large and small opened up around the province, and communities began gathering in the treasures that illustrate their former way of life and significant events in their history.

Today, museums can be found in all parts of Nova Scotia. Some of these have a specialized theme, like the Margaree Salmon Museum, the Maritime Museum of the Atlantic in Halifax, or the Joggins Fossil Centre. Others present with pride a variety of objects that tell the story of their community, its personalities, or special events. The items in their collections, whether large or small, provide tangible links to our province's history and culture. Museums often begin with a heritage or historical society looking for a way to preserve objects that represent their community's past. Sometimes a small personal or family collection can form the nucleus of a museum. Additional items are then added as members of the community recognize the importance of some of the objects they have stored away. Some large institutions can afford to purchase important items, but most museums depend on donations of artefacts from people's homes, barns, or workshops. Not everything can be displayed at once, and many museums keep material in storage that can be brought out for a special exhibit.

An object in a museum may never have had a great deal of monetary value, but it can provide insight into the lives of those who used it. Items like a diary, an article of clothing, chinaware, a sword, or a butter churn all have stories to tell about their owners and environments. I have selected fifty of the treasures that have led me to a deeper understanding of their stories. They are presented in a generally chronological order, and range in date from pre-history to the present day. Each item I have selected has a fascinating story to tell, and their stories have taken me on a journey. I invite you to share this journey with me.

Fossilized amphibian

315 MILLION YEARS AGO

Joggins Fossil Centre

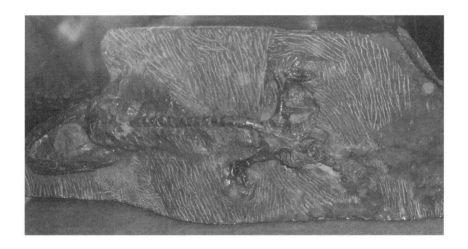

THIS SMALL EARLY AMPHIBIAN, WHOSE FOSSILIZED SKELETON is embedded in this piece of Carboniferous rock, wandered through the forest that covered Joggins, Nova Scotia, some 315 million years ago—1 million years before dinosaurs began to roam the earth. Known to scientists as *Dendrerpeton acadianum*, this creature belonged to a group of amphibians and reptiles known as tetrapods, which were comfortable on land and in water. This item is now on loan from the Nova Scotia Museum to the Fossil Centre at Joggins, the amphibian's original home.

Today the many-layered cliffs at Joggins attract visitors from all over the world, including professional scientists, students, tourists, and the general public. The exposed strata in the cliff formations represent the history of the so-called "Coal Age" or Carboniferous period, when sediments that would later become coal were laid down. Fossilized amphibians from this period represent the development of early life forms, like fish and sea creatures, as they emerged from the water and began to adapt to life on land.

In those days, the Joggins area was part of a larger continental land mass known today as Pangea, which later split apart to form what are now North and South America and Africa. The Bay of Fundy had not yet been formed. Both the region's landscape and creatures were very different from the vegetation and wildlife that call the area home today. It was a swampy rainforest, featuring trees known as lycopsids, which were huge versions (30 metres high and up to 1 metre in diameter) of some contemporary mosses, as well as giant horsetails and ferns. These plants absorbed large quantities of carbon dioxide from the atmosphere, and as they died off they rotted down to form beds of peat that later hardened into coal.

The climate varied over the years. From time to time, flood water overwhelmed the area. The resulting sediments hardened to form the layers of sandstone and shale that run diagonally across the cliff face today, interspersed with the coal seams. In these layers of sedimentary rock are preserved the remains of both the plant and the animal life of that moment in time: tree trunks, some still upright; impressions of fern leaves, animal tracks, ripples—and even raindrops—on the sand; and the skeletons and droppings of long-extinct animals, like our little amphibian. These are the fossils found in the rocks today.

The "coal cliffs" at Joggins were known from the early days of European settlement and appear on maps dating back to the early 1700s. Scientists, in turn, were attracted to the area beginning in the late 1820s, partly because of the development of the coal industry in Nova Scotia. But it was the fossil trees that excited the imagination of men like famed geologist

Sir Charles Lyell, who first visited the cliffs in 1842 and returned ten years later in the company of a young Pictou geologist, William Dawson. The two men were particularly interested in the tree remains that could be seen in the cliff face, preserved where they had grown by the various layers of sedimentary rock formed around them. But they also found, in an unexpected place, evidence of the animal life developing at that time. In the interior of a hollow fossil tree they came upon a partial skeleton that proved to be that of a tetrapod very similar to the one depicted here.

Dawson went on to work in the field of paleontology, returning to Joggins and finding many more fragmentary specimens of amphibians and reptiles in the hollow trunks of these ancient trees. Dawson's specimens were broken skeletons, but the present example, found at the Joggins cliffs in 1987 by two McGill University students, is more complete. It, too, is a tetrapod, a long-extinct ancestor of the reptiles we know today, such as lizards, turtles, and crocodiles. It is embedded in the fossilized remains of the tree in which it ended its days. There are many theories about how these creatures came to be there: Did they fall into broken trees partially buried by sediment? Were they washed in by floods? Or did they use the trees as dens or hiding places from fire or predators, entering through fissures in the trunk?

The strong Bay of Fundy tides cause continuous erosion of the cliffs, which means that new fossils are constantly being exposed and discovered. The Joggins Fossil Institute is an important centre for study and research, and the Fossil Centre, opened in 2008—the same year the Joggins Fossil Cliffs was designated a UNESCO World Heritage Site—provides an excellent public interpretation of the fossil record and the geological history of the area. Visitors are offered a guided tour and a chance to observe for themselves the items exposed in the cliffs and on the beach. Who knows? You too may make a discovery as significant as this little fossil.

2

Mi'kmaw arrowhead

400+ YEARS AGO

DesBrisay Museum, Bridgewater

 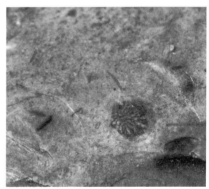

T HIS STONE ARROWHEAD, WITH ITS MYSTERIOUS INCLUSION,
formed part of a collection assembled by Mather Byles DesBrisay
in the second half of the nineteenth century. It brings together
the stories of the aboriginal people who have lived in what they know as
Mi'kma'ki—the Maritime provinces and Gaspé peninsula—for over ten
thousand years and a nineteenth-century antiquarian with a passion for
historical and exotic objects.

DesBrisay came to Bridgewater in 1865 and opened his law practice
there. An ambitious man, he would go on to represent Lunenburg County
in the House of Assembly for some years, serving for a short time as
Speaker, before resigning to take up his appointment as County Court

Judge. Judge DesBrisay had an interest in history from his student days, when he wrote a prizewinning essay on the history of Lunenburg County. (He went on to publish a valuable book on the same subject.) And he was also a collector of interesting objects.

Before the development of modern archaeological methods and environmentally controlled museums, collections of old or exotic items were often displayed in private homes for the enjoyment of the collectors and their friends. The DesBrisay home on Pleasant Street in Bridgewater was full of objects that formed the judge's collection, and it attracted many visitors. Among the items displayed were Mi'kmaw artefacts from a site not far from DesBrisay's home, some of which he had found personally, as he documents in his *History of the County of Lunenburg*: "Remains of pottery, parts of pans and other vessels (with curved rims, full of marks or indentations, each different from the rest), a stone pipe, lead (of two pounds' weight), a very small clay bottle, with fluted sides and rude glazing at the mouth, and a lot of arrow-heads were discovered (some by the writer) in 1877, at Koch's [Cooks] Falls, near Bridgewater." The objects gathered here by Judge DesBrisay were not subject to scientific analysis, as they would be had they been found by archaeologists today, but his account clearly establishes this site as one of the places on the river where a Mi'kmaw encampment was located.

The Mi'kmaq had known the LaHave River and its watershed long before Europeans came to North America. Family groups had established dwelling sites on its banks and tributaries, hunted in its forests, and caught fish in its waters. The river was used as a route for trade and for seasonal migration between the interior of the province and the estuary, where, when summer came, the Mi'kmaq gathered clams and mussels and fished. Champlain recorded Mi'kmaw encampments at Petite Rivière and on the east bank of the LaHave in the early seventeenth century, and archaeologists have found evidence of a number of sites along the river where they set up their wigwams and inevitably left behind traces of their presence. Signs of Mi'kmaw site use may include fireplaces, fish weirs, middens where shells and animal bones were discarded, and artefacts that tell us something of the former way of life of Nova Scotia's First Nations. Among the best preserved of these objects are the stone tools and weapons that were manufactured and used by the Mi'kmaq for thousands of years. These include knives, spearheads, and arrowheads.

This arrowhead probably dates back at least 400 years, to before or soon after contact between the Mi'kmaq and early Europeans. The Mi'kmaq made pointed weapons by chipping flakes from a piece of stone using a harder stone tool until the desired shape—the arrowhead—was achieved. The arrowheads were then attached to long shafts, with a thong or spruce root bound around notches at each side, to form weapons for hunters or warriors.

The animals killed by Mi'kmaw hunters formed an important part of their people's diet, and also provided skins for basic clothing and furs for warmth in winter. European fishermen who visited our shores by the second half of the sixteenth century exchanged with the Mi'kmaq iron implements like knives and axes for the furs they would sell back home. European trading companies were later formed specifically to acquire furs, particularly beaver pelts for the manufacture of the hats in fashion at that time. The Mi'kmaq were happy to receive iron implements and weapons in exchange, and the manufacture of stone tools gradually died out.

In this and other ways, the Europeans' arrival spelled the beginning of the end of a way of life on the LaHave. When the French established a settlement at Fort Point in 1632, they formed good relations with the Mi'kmaq and introduced them to the Catholic faith and European customs. With few French women among the early settlers, a number of marriages took place between settlers and aboriginal women. A 1708 French census of Mi'kmaq living in the LaHave area, including Merliguesche (now Lunenburg), lists a French baptismal name for every Mi'kmaq and records several mixed marriages. Not surprisingly, in the struggle between the French and the British for control of Nova Scotia, the Mi'kmaq sided with the French. Despite an initial mutual hostility between British settlers and the Mi'kmaq, in 1725 the first of several peace treaties was signed, though for many years the Mi'kmaq were marginalized. Today, though their descendants are reviving their culture, the Mi'kmaq paddle their canoes on the LaHave only on ceremonial occasions.

After Judge DesBrisay's death in 1900, his widow sold his collection to the town of Bridgewater. After being transferred to the courthouse, the collection was subsequently cared for by the Women's Institute in a building on King Street. It then spent a few years in storage before being permanently housed in the DesBrisay Museum. Sadly, some of the artefacts the judge mentioned have disappeared, but this arrowhead, among other objects from his collection, remind us of the pre-contact culture of the Mi'kmaw nation.

3

Porcupine-quill box

C. 1900

Queens County Museum, Liverpool

BEFORE CONTACT WITH EUROPEANS, THE MI'KMAQ MADE USE of the earth's natural resources for all their needs. They subsisted on the foods found in their environment, hunting the native animals of the area, fishing in its rivers and bays, and gathering the wild fruits of its fields and forests. No portion of an animal was wasted. The meat was used for food, skins were made into leather clothing, and furs were used for winter warmth. Even the lowly porcupine—considered a nuisance by many people today and scorned by modern hunters—served its purpose: its meat went into the cooking pot, and its quills were put to practical use for decoration.

Mi'kmaw women were highly skilled in enhancing their leather garments, moccasins, pouches, and other items with colourful traditional motifs. Among the basic materials incorporated in their designs were porcupine quills. They were proficient in extracting the quills from the animals' skin, which most of us would consider a dangerous and daunting task. Once extracted, they prepared the quills by cleaning and softening them, and, because the quills are naturally white with darker tips, the women coloured them with natural dyes made from plants and minerals. They then used the quills, sometimes in combination with other materials, to decorate their clothing as well as domestic items such as birchbark bowls, boxes, and baskets. The Mi'kmaq were well known for their artistry, and, because of the quality of their quillwork, were sometimes referred to as the "Porcupine People."

When European fishermen and traders first crossed the Atlantic, their commercial dealings with the Mi'kmaq were concentrated on acquiring the furs so highly valued in Europe. By the time the French began to settle in Acadie, decorative items made by aboriginal women were also being offered as trade goods. Nicolas Denys travelled extensively in what are now the Maritime provinces and, at the end of the seventeenth century, wrote an account of the Mi'kmaq that included interesting details of their crafts and their trade. He described little leather bags, or "*peschipotys*," for which "the Indian women fix the price to fishermen according to the kind of skin and its fantastic ornamentation…made from Porcupine quills." Denys also wrote of Mi'kmaw dishes made of bark, some of which were also decorated with quills, using the same technique to make boxes like this example, which is held in the Queens County Museum on loan from the Nova Scotia Museum. The ornamentation of this box, which is estimated to date from the early twentieth century, incorporates traditional motifs handed down from generation to generation.

During the eighteenth century the fur trade dwindled and beaver hats ceased to be fashionable. Fishermen no longer crossed the Atlantic seasonally with trade goods, but lived in settled communities in Nova Scotia, often encroaching on traditional native hunting and fishing grounds. The lives of the Mi'kmaq were also changing, as they, too, adopted a more sedentary lifestyle. Commercial transactions took place increasingly in cash rather than in kind. Fewer Mi'kmaw garments were made of leather and more of the cloth bought from town merchants. The women continued to decorate them, but now used purchased beads and ribbons more often than quills.

The art of working with porcupine quills did not die out, however. The Mi'kmaq increasingly used their traditional skills to make decorative articles for sale to the non-native population as well as—or instead of—ornamenting their own clothing. As time went on, although Nova Scotians no longer bought beaver pelts, they eagerly purchased native craft objects. Among the items that the Mi'kmaq women brought to market in the nineteenth century to sell to town-dwellers were the baskets for which they are famous, and quill-decorated items like this box, which is a beautiful example of their skill. The chevron pattern on the sides and the geometric shapes on the top are traditional designs, which also often included squares, diamonds, and stars, found in varying combinations in many decorative items of Mi'kmaw craft. The intricate patterns on the top include white quills woven or overlaid on a coloured background, and the band at the side of the lid incorporates a traditional woven motif.

Items of this kind were very popular during the Victorian period, but as time went on many traditional native skills were abandoned by the Mi'kmaq, who preferred to seek occupations more in line with those of the rest of the population. The art of decorating birchbark with porcupine quills survived for some time, but by the end of the twentieth century it was in danger of dying out along with other traditional crafts.

Successful efforts have been made recently to revive and nurture these skills. Mi'kmaw baskets remain popular items among the public, and porcupine quills are an attractive component of Mi'kmaw jewellery, where they are incorporated into beautiful earrings and necklaces, using both traditional and modern materials. A few Mi'kmaq still preserve the skill, passed down through generations, of making porcupine quill birchbark boxes like this one. In the twenty-first century, workshops offered in Mi'kmaw cultural centres have renewed interest in learning traditional skills, and the ancient art of quillwork is being learned by a new generation of craftspeople.

～ 4 ～

Beaver pelt and hat

REPLICA OF 17TH-CENTURY DESIGN

Port Royal National Historic Site

THE TWO MOST VALUABLE EXPORTS FROM NOVA SCOTIA AT THE beginning of the seventeenth century were fish and furs. European fishermen crossed the Atlantic every summer to harvest cod from the banks off the east coast, where they obtained furs from the Mi'kmaq in exchange for manufactured goods. Soon companies were formed to operate the fur trade, and the hottest market in Europe was for beaver pelts. The pelts were made into hats like this, much in demand among European gentlemen of the time. Neither these hats nor pelts have survived the ravages of time, but similar recently made items symbolize the resources for which nations once fought and over which lives were lost.

Trading rights within the area of North America nominally controlled by the French king were granted to those in his favour. In 1604 a company headed by trader and colonist Pierre Du Gua de Monts obtained the monopoly for the fur trade in Acadia. It was de Monts's intention to establish a permanent settlement here to protect his interests and to maintain a year-round French presence in the region. Accompanied by François Gravé Du Pont, Jean de Poutrincourt, Samuel de Champlain, and other gentlemen, de Monts crossed the Atlantic with a team of tradesmen and labourers and explored the coast of Nova Scotia and the Bay of Fundy in search of a suitable site for this settlement. Their first choice, Saint Croix Island, on what is now the boundary between New Brunswick and Maine, proved disastrous. In the spring of 1605, after losing many men to scurvy over the bitter winter, the survivors re-established themselves at a spot on the north shore of the Annapolis Basin. They named it Port Royal.

The settlement here was more successful. The men constructed the Port Royal Habitation in the lee of the North Mountain around a courtyard, where the walls of the buildings provided protection from the wind and weather, and, importantly, they established friendly relations with the local Mi'kmaq through their chief, Membertou. De Monts then returned to France to represent the company's interests there, leaving Du Pont in charge, assisted by Champlain. Their task was to establish a successful commercial enterprise and build up a viable community. With the help of their aboriginal neighbours, they survived the winter with fewer casualties, and once again set up a trading post.

The reconstruction of the Habitation, based on Champlain's description and his plan of Port Royal, gives some insight into life in those early days of settlement. We see the workmen's quarters with the dining hall on the main floor, the house of Gravé Du Pont and Champlain and other gentlemen's accommodation, the forge and the kitchen, and along one side of the quadrangle, the store where the Mi'kmaq brought their furs for trading. Here the beaver pelts would be sorted and stacked into bales, to be shipped back to France where Sieur de Monts hoped to sell them profitably to eager hat makers.

Having accompanied de Monts in the spring of 1604, Jean de Poutrincourt returned to France that same fall with a shipload of furs. Early in 1606 the king named him seigneur of Port Royal and in the spring of that year, with his son Charles de Biencourt, Poutrincourt led a fresh contingent of settlers to the Habitation. He would consolidate the settlement and take charge of the trading post for de Monts. New developments quickly got under way. Poutrincourt began to cultivate the fertile land on the point where Annapolis Royal now stands and oversaw the construction of a watermill on what is now Allains River, running into the Annapolis Basin, to process the wheat he grew there. To ease the hardships of winter, Champlain in 1606 established the Order of Good Cheer, aimed at boosting health and morale. The gentlemen took it in turns to provide the evening's entertainment by hunting fresh game, preparing the meal, and serving it ceremoniously. By the spring of 1606, Port Royal was beginning to develop from an isolated trading post into a self-sufficient settlement.

Unfortunately this was not to last.

The monopoly granted to de Monts's company was hard to enforce, and independent fishermen and traders often poached in his territory. As a result, profits from the sale of furs had not accrued as rapidly as de Monts's backers had hoped, and they began to withdraw their support. At the same time, rival merchants resented the granting of de Monts's monopoly and persuaded the king to cancel it. At the end of the summer of 1607, the settlers were forced to withdraw from Port Royal and return to France, leaving the Habitation in the care of Chief Membertou.

But Jean de Poutrincourt still had faith in the potential of Port Royal. He raised money, and by 1610 was able to finance another expedition. He returned to take up possession of the land he had been granted. He found the Habitation in good condition, and began once more to cultivate the land at the head of the basin and resume trading. Poutrincourt was able to send a shipload of furs back to France at the end of the season, but his supply ship was delayed the following spring and he had to return to France to seek further assistance. During his long absence, Poutrincourt's son's mismanagement and discord among the clergy had weakened the settlement.

In 1613, while Poutrincourt was still in France, Port Royal fell victim to international rivalry between the English and French for control of the North Atlantic fish and fur trade. An English raid led by Samuel Argall destroyed the Habitation while its inhabitants worked in the fields. When Poutrincourt returned the following spring, he found the place in ruins and the settlers starving. He took most of them back to France. His son, Charles de Biencourt, remained, however, with his friend Charles de Saint-Étienne de La Tour. After a few more years' struggle to maintain the fur trade, Biencourt died in 1623. La Tour abandoned the settlement and went on to operate a trading post at Cape Sable, sending beaver pelts back to France for many years. He was to play a major role in the history of Acadie.

~ 5 ~

French brick

1632

Fort Point Museum, LaHave

THIS IS A FAIRLY ORDINARY LOOKING RED CLAY BRICK, BUT it has a long history. Its journey began in Auray, Brittany, on July 4, 1632, in the hold of one of three ships headed into the North Atlantic. The leader of this expedition was Isaac de Razilly, who carried with him aboard *l'Espérance en Dieu* a commission from King Louis XIII to establish a settlement in the king's name. At this time, France and England were still vying for control of the valuable North American fur trade and fishing grounds. Champlain's settlement in Quebec had fallen to the British three years previously, but New France, as French territory in North America was then called, had been returned by treaty to the French crown in the spring of 1632.

Razilly was a naval officer, a commander of the Order of Malta, a member of the Company of New France, and an associate of Samuel de Champlain. Having distinguished himself through naval actions off the French coast during the Wars of Religion (1562–1598), he received the call in March 1632—while combating piracy in the Mediterranean—to establish a settlement in the Atlantic region of New France known as Acadie. A small French population had existed in Acadie since the days of de Monts's arrival at Port Royal in 1605, but after English raids destroyed the original settlement, the French presence was reduced to Charles de La Tour's small community in the Cape Sable area. Sir William Alexander had installed a Scottish garrison at Port Royal in 1629 and planned a colony in what he called Nova Scotia, but only three years later the territory was restored to France.

That July Razilly set sail for Acadie on behalf of the king and the Company of New France, with a colonizing party of some three hundred men. Some would remain in Canso to man a fort there, while others would proceed to Port Royal—some to replace the Scottish garrison and others to escort its members back to Britain. On September 8, 1632, the main party, consisting of two hundred men under Razilly's leadership, sailed into the harbour Champlain had named *Port de LaHève* (now Green Bay) at the mouth of the LaHave River. The party continued upriver to a point of land jutting out on the western side, commanding a view of the estuary. Here they came ashore and unloaded their supplies, including the bricks that had been stowed as ballast; these would serve another purpose now that the ships had reached their destination. Later, Razilly wrote that he had brought with him construction material consisting of "lime, plaster, bricks, 2,000 planks and all necessary tools."

We do not know the details of the construction that took place at what is now LaHave, but clearly Razilly's first concern was to provide shelter for the new arrivals. It was already late in the year, and Champlain's experiences in New France would have alerted him to the kind of weather they might expect. Even so, there were some deaths that first winter. But by the second winter, living conditions had improved and the colonists lived comfortably. The main buildings consisted of the stoutly walled Fort Sainte Marie de Grace, overlooking the seaward approaches. The settlement also comprised dwellings for the colonists and a chapel where the Capuchin fathers who had accompanied them held services and preached Christianity to the native inhabitants of the area. Our brick is believed to have come from a building in the fort, perhaps the governor's quarters or one of the dwelling houses.

Once the initial construction period was over, most of the contracted artisans returned to France, to be replaced by farmers and tradesmen from western France who would form the permanent settlement. These men cleared and cultivated land, and Nicolas Denys started a lumbering business on the eastern side of the river. In April 1636 the *St-Jean* left La Rochelle in western France with a new band of colonists, including women and children, destined for the place we now call LaHave. Their stay there was to be brief; however, Isaac de Razilly died in early July of that year, four years after leaving France. His second-in-command, Charles de Menou d'Aulnay, took charge of the colony.

D'Aulnay was familiar with the Bay of Fundy and considered the former French settlement of Port Royal a more suitable place to establish the administrative centre of Acadie. So LaHève was abandoned. In 1654 its buildings would be burnt to the ground as a result of conflicts among rival French businessmen vying for control of the fishery and fur trade.

Gradually, the tides and currents eroded the point on which the fort stood. In the late nineteenth century, Judge M. B. DesBrisay wrote:

> The ruins of the fort and of the chapel are distinctly visible. The outer bank of the point yet contains a portion of the wall built up by the French, and judging from what is left, it must have been a substantial piece of masonry…. It would seem, from the mounds still visible, that the fort must have been of large size and that other buildings had been erected in its immediate

neighbourhood—perhaps the residences of the Governor and other officers. Inside the fort wall, on the side nearest the sea, were seen some years since, the ruins of the magazine.

Erosion continued, and by the early twentieth century only part of the fort's wall and the chapel foundation were visible. A cairn was erected in 1929 with a plaque marking the area as a national historic site. By mid-century, storms, tides, and currents had carried away every remnant of construction on Fort Point except for some material lying on the beach below the cliff. Our brick, one of many found there in the twentieth century, is now on display in Fort Point Museum. To this day, it tells the story of a courageous band of colonists who came to this New World outpost in the earliest days of settlement, to whom several Acadian families can trace their ancestry.

6

D'Aulnay stone

1651

Fort Anne National Historic Site, Annapolis Royal

ARCHAEOLOGISTS DISCOVERED THIS STONE, BEARING THE inscription *JOSEPH DE MENOU SIEUR DONES 1651*, during excavations that took place from 1989 to 1992 at the Fort Anne site in Annapolis Royal. It provides a direct link with the family of Charles de Menou d'Aulnay, the man who administered Acadia following the death of Isaac de Razilly in 1636, revived the French settlement at Port Royal, and became governor in 1647.

D'Aulnay came to Acadie in 1632 as the lieutenant of his cousin, Isaac de Razilly, who had established his headquarters at LaHève. Travelling back and forth from LaHève to France with shiploads of fish or furs, d'Aulnay negotiated their sale, organized supplies, and recruited colonists in collaboration with Razilly's brother and business associate, Claude de Launay Rasilly, who remained in France but received grants at LaHève and Port Royal.

In 1635 d'Aulnay recaptured the French trading post at Pentaguet (on Maine's lower Penobscot River) that had been seized by the English. The following year, two events took place that would prove significant for him. Firstly, early that summer the *St-Jean* arrived at LaHève with a contingent of settlers and a party of gentry, including Nicolas Le Creux, Razilly's lieutenant at Canso, his wife, Anne, her brothers, and her sister, Jeanne Motin. And secondly, on July 6, Isaac de Razilly died and d'Aulnay took charge of the settlement on behalf of Claude de Launay Rasilly. Soon afterwards, d'Aulnay began to transfer the inhabitants of LaHève to Port Royal, which he considered a better location from which to defend Acadie against attack from New England. He built the settlement not at the site of the former Habitation, but on the point of land where Poutrincourt had established a farm. It was here that the Scots had constructed a fort and Razilly maintained a small garrison. Strategically, this was a good choice: Port Royal lay between the Annapolis and Allains Rivers and commanded a view down the basin towards the gut, through which any invading ships would have to pass. D'Aulnay's fort replaced the Scottish one, and would in turn be replaced by others, the last of which would be Fort Anne.

From 1632 until Isaac de Razilly's death in 1636, control of the colony of Acadie had been divided between Razilly and Charles de La Tour. La Tour, who lived and traded in the Cape Sable area southwest of Port Royal for many years, also had a concession on the Saint John River, while Razilly controlled LaHève and Port Royal. While those two men had coexisted peacefully, LaTour and d'Aulnay disliked each other and were unwilling to co-operate. D'Aulnay had also made an enemy of Nicolas Denys, a merchant from Tours, France, who had come to Acadie with Isaac de Razilly and established a lumbering business and fishing stations. These hostilities were to cause many years of turmoil in Acadie. In 1638 the king named d'Aulnay lieutenant general, a title formerly held by Razilly; this did nothing to improve d'Aulnay's relationships with his rivals. In the same year, d'Aulnay married Jeanne Motin. They would have eight children, including Joseph, whose name appears on this stone.

Once established at Port Royal, d'Aulnay refurbished the fort and settlement and brought in more colonists, many of whom are ancestors of today's Acadians. He continued to maintain the post at Pentaguet and laid a solid foundation for the colony at Port Royal; unfortunately his administration was marked by skirmishes both with d'Aulnay's French rivals and the English merchants in Boston who supported La Tour. D'Aulnay's dispute with La Tour escalated, culminating in 1645 when he attacked and seized La Tour's fort at Saint John in his absence. A number of the defenders were killed, and La Tour's wife, Françoise-Marie Jacquelin, who had led the defence, was imprisoned and died shortly afterwards.

D'Aulnay died in a canoe accident in 1650, deeply indebted to French merchant Emmanuel Le Borgne. His eldest son, Joseph, inherited the title of seigneur at about eleven years of age. Joseph's grandfather, René de Menou, became the d'Aulnay children's legal guardian, but he was in France and could do little to assist. It was left to d'Aulnay's widow to take immediate steps to protect her children. The following year, one of the stones incorporated in the entrance to the fort was engraved with Joseph's name and the title of *Sieur Dones* (d'Aulnay). In her *History of Port Royal/Annapolis Royal, 1605–1800*, author Brenda Dunn attributes the engraving to Jeanne Motin, who she believes had the words carved into the stone in order to emphasize the rights of Menou's heirs in the colony.

Despite having made this claim, Jeanne now found herself in a very dangerous position. In an isolated settlement far from France, with rival contenders vying for control of the colony, its fur trade, and fishery, she and her family were very much at the mercy of the ruthless men around her. The problem was solved in an unlikely fashion: the widow Motin became the wife of her husband's hated rival, Charles de La Tour. Considered objectively, this was an ideal solution for both parties. Motin obtained security—or as much as could be expected in those turbulent times—for herself and her children. La Tour obtained the allegiance of d'Aulnay's supporters, who might otherwise have continued the feud. This marriage of convenience between Jeanne Motin and Charles de La Tour produced five children.

We hear little more of Joseph. He did not participate in the subsequent struggles for control of Acadie. After some years at Port Royal with their mother, he and his siblings travelled to France, where Joseph became a military officer. Today only this stone remains to remind us of the presence in Acadie of the young Sieur de Menou d'Aulnay.

～7～

Acadian-style dyking spade

1935, BASED ON 17TH-CENTURY DESIGN

Avon River Heritage Museum, Newport Landing

THIS SPADE IS QUITE DIFFERENT FROM THE ones we use to dig our gardens—its narrow blade would not serve very well to turn over the potato patch. It is in fact a very specialized tool, the design of which goes back a long way. Implements like this have been made and used in Nova Scotia since the seventeenth century, and in France likely even before then. Unfortunately, the original Acadian dyking spades have mostly been broken or have long since rotted away. This example, on display at the Avon River Heritage Museum, is one of fifty made by Graham Knowles in 1935 based on the original design. Such a tool would have been familiar to the earliest European settlers along the banks of the Avon River. It represents a system of reclaiming marshland for agriculture known as dyking, which was introduced to Nova Scotia in the seventeenth century and survives in some regions to this day.

The rivers flowing into the Bay of Fundy and Minas

Basin run through marshlands that have been built up by sediment deposited by the rivers and tides. The Acadians who settled here were familiar with the methods of dyking and draining coastal marshland used in western France to create fields and pastures. Dykes prevent salt water from flooding the land at high tide, and a drainage system allows the rain and melting snow gradually to cleanse the soil of salt, leaving behind fertile farmland. Dyke construction was a skill that French settlers had brought with them to North America, and one that the Acadians practiced as they moved from Port Royal to the shores of the Minas Basin and its rivers.

The Acadian villages consisted mainly of members of one or more extended families, who worked together to reclaim the surrounding marshland for farming. The dykes they constructed consisted of a core of earth, sometimes reinforced with brush or logs, built up to a height of about 1.5 metres. They were then faced with sods cut from the surrounding salt marshes, where the grass, known as cord grass, has long, strong roots that combine with the heavy soil to form a dense mass. Specialized dyking spades like this one were designed to cut blocks the width of the blade out of this amalgam of roots and earth. These blocks were dried and used like bricks to create an impermeable surface for the protective dykes.

The dykes kept the salt water from flooding over the land at high tide, but they would also retain the fresh water from brooks and drainage ditches unless some provision was made to allow this water to escape at low tide. This was done by installing aboiteaux, wood-lined passages through the dykes, each of which was equipped with a *clapet*, a wooden flap mounted at the top, which would swing open at low tide allowing fresh water to flow through but would be closed by the pressure of salt water from outside as the tide rose. The remains of several aboiteaux have been found in recent years.

Many thousands of acres of farmland were created in this way during the period of Acadian settlement, from the mid-1600s until the Deportation of 1755. The area known as Grand Pré, between the Cornwallis and Gaspereau Rivers, is probably the best-known example of this form of agriculture. A string of family villages also grew up along the Pisiquid (Avon) River. Houses were built on higher ground above the dyked farmland in case of accidental flooding, and there was also some farming on upland areas.

Five years after the Deportation, settlers from New England known as Planters were brought in to replace the Acadian farmers and to revive agriculture in this part of Nova Scotia. On the Avon River, a contingent of New Englanders from Newport, Rhode Island, arrived at what is now known as Newport Landing. Chief Surveyor Charles Morris, who laid out the Township of Newport (originally named Falmouth East), estimated that by 1762 about seventy families were settled there, living and farming on the old Acadian lands.

The Acadians had not only built the dykes, they also maintained them. Various officials complained from time to time that the Acadians' reliance on drained marshes rather than cleared uplands was a sign of laziness, but their upkeep required constant vigilance and hard work. Although the dykes were strong and high enough to cope with normal high tides, storms and abnormal rainfall could damage them, and from time to time work parties were sent out to repair them, cutting new sods when necessary with their specialized spades. The Planter settlers on the Bay of Fundy were unfamiliar with the art of dyke building and maintenance. It was not long before flooding occurred, and they began to realize that their crops and their livelihood were in danger. An urgent call for help went out, and the authorities were forced to allow some Acadians who had escaped deportation to assist the newcomers.

The British eventually learned from the Acadians how to maintain the dykes, and also became successful farmers, shipbuilders, and seamen. They used traditional methods and tools for many years to work on the dykes, which can still be seen today. In the twentieth century increased mechanization allowed new methods to supersede the old ways and built bigger, stronger structures. But as late as 1935, fifty of these spades were made in the traditional design, a remnant of the ancient practice of dyke building by human labour.

～ 8 ～

Acadian millstone

1660–1688

Musée des Acadiens des Pubnicos et Centre de recherche,

West Pubnico

THIS ROUGHLY CIRCULAR STONE, PIERCED BY A SQUARE HOLE, was found at East Pubnico and is now in the Musée des Acadiens at West Pubnico. Though it is now in poor condition, this artefact appears to be a grinding stone, or millstone, of a gristmill. Historians date it back to a very early period of the West Pubnico Acadian settlement, where a gristmill is known to have existed before 1688. The water-powered mill produced flour by grinding or crushing the grain produced on the manor lands and in the surrounding area between two stones, one rotating and one stationary.

Pubnico is said to be the oldest community in Canada still populated by descendants of the founding settlers. This land in the Cape Sable area was granted as a barony to Philippe Mius d'Entremont in 1653 by Charles de La Tour, the king's lieutenant in this area, and within a few years the Mius d'Entremont family was well established. Their territory was known by its Mi'kmaw name, Pobomcoup, and extended from Cape Negro (Barrington) to Cape Fourchu (Yarmouth). The same families have occupied the area surrounding Pubnico Harbour almost continuously since 1653—the only exception being the disastrous period in the mid-1750s known as the Expulsion of the Acadians, or *Le Grand Dérangement*, when British troops drove the inhabitants from their lands.

Philippe Mius d'Entremont arrived from France with his wife, Madelaine Hélie, and their daughter, Marie-Marguerite. Four more children were born in Acadie. He also recruited settlers and cleared and farmed the land on the east side of Pubnico Harbour, which became the centre of population in that region. Although Philippe initiated the development of the settlement, on his appointment as attorney general to the King in 1670 he was occupied with his official duties in Port Royal. So it was left to his eldest son, Jacques Muis d'Entremont, to maintain the family home at the centre of the settlement and to take charge of its affairs. Before the end of the seventeenth century, Jacques had built a manor house and a church, and a gristmill had been established on a brook running into the east side of the harbour.

Jacques married one of Charles de La Tour's daughters, Anne de St-Étienne de La Tour, and his next-youngest brother, Abraham, married her sister, Marguerite. Both men had large families, and the d'Entremont name remains the most common one in the Pubnico region. By the early eighteenth century, the third son, Philippe Mius d'Entremont, was married to a Mi'kmaw woman and lived in Merliguesche (Lunenburg) where the family was known as Mius. Philippe's many descendants retained the Mius name, with variations in spelling. The elder daughter, Marie-Marguerite, married Pierre Melanson, the patriarch of Grand Pré. A second daughter, Madeleine, appears to have remained unmarried.

In 1699 Governor Villebon visited Pubnico from St. Jean and described the d'Entremont establishment in a memoir to French officials. He found it had good farmland and fishing; Jacques, his wife and eight children were living at the manor, their peas and grain were flourishing, and they had "thirty cattle, three sheep, eighteen pigs and a water mill." This grinding stone is probably all that remains of the water mill. The growth of the settlement was, however, halted by the Expulsion of the Acadians, which began in the mid-1750s.

Although they were not among the first contingent of deportees, the members of the d'Entremont household were sent to Massachusetts in 1758, after more than one hundred years in Pubnico, and their settlement was burnt to the ground. Jacques d'Entremont died in exile, but his family and several others—the Amirault, Belliveau, Duon (d'Éon) and Mius families—came back to the Cape Sable area in 1767. On their return, the d'Entremonts found English settlers in possession of some of their land, including the manor site, but they re-established their family on the opposite side of the harbour, at what is now West Pubnico. The descendants of Jacques d'Entremont still form the majority of the population of this community.

The early Acadian settlement at East Pubnico seemed to have been wiped off the map, but in the 1990s, with the discovery of the remnants of an aboiteau, archaeologists began to take an interest in the probable manor site. In 1996 excavations were carried out on the hill where the house was thought to have stood. The following summer, two Acadians were exploring the area closer to the water when a visiting archaeologist mentioned seeing what appeared to be a millstone at the edge of the brook that runs into the harbour nearby. When they located it, it was partially sunk in the mud, and covered by water at high tide.

Although it cannot be proved beyond doubt that the stone is connected to the mill Villebon described, it is extremely likely. In Europe, it was common for the local seigneur to run a gristmill to which his tenants would bring their grain, and this mill would have followed that tradition. The stone is badly worn, damaged, or unfinished, and while it is not perfectly round, it has the characteristic features of a millstone: a hole in the middle and traces of striations on the flat side. Its location beside the brook that powered Jacques d'Entremont's mill supports the belief that this stone was made in the seventeenth century, making the millstone a rare survival from the pre-deportation period.

Many generations later, the inhabitants of Pubnico treasure this and other reminders of the unique history of their community. It is now displayed in the Musée des Acadiens, along with the aboiteau that was part of the drainage system on the nearby salt marsh. Both are valuable reminders of the early days of French settlement in Nova Scotia.

~ 9 ~

Key to Fort Anne

1710

Fort Anne National Historic Site, Annapolis Royal

THIS MASSIVE KEY DISPLAYED AT THE NATIONAL HISTORIC
Site of Fort Anne symbolizes a defining event in Nova Scotia's
history and in the checkered history of the fort itself.

Leading up to 1710, there had been a century of sporadic fighting
between the French and the British for control of the natural resources of
Acadie/Nova Scotia. For most of this time, fighting was concentrated on
its main settlement and administrative centre, Port Royal, at the head of
the Annapolis Basin. There had been other forts here previously. Raiders
from New England had destroyed the earliest French settlement, the
Habitation described by Champlain. The site was then occupied from
1629 to 1632 by a Scottish garrison, which established Charles Fort at
the head of the Annapolis Basin. The new structure built in its place in
the late 1630s by Charles de Menou d'Aulnay was renewed by successive
French administrations.

Control of Acadie/Nova Scotia changed hands several times over the years, often as part of treaties settling European disputes. In 1654 Port Royal was captured by an expedition from New England, giving Britain nominal ownership of the colony. In 1667, when the Treaty of Breda returned mainland Nova Scotia to France, Port Royal and its fort were once again under French control. The matter was by no means settled, however. Lacking regular supplies from France, Acadian residents remained dependent on trade with the New England merchants who continued to operate stores in Port Royal. As tension between Britain and France increased during the 1680s, the town's population was augmented by the presence of French officials and soldiers, who now formed the majority of the population. At this point, many early Acadian inhabitants had left town and were now settled on their farms higher up the river. The church, the governor's house, the house of the seigneur, Alexandre Le Borgne, and the British merchants' premises were the most important buildings. D'Aulnay's fort was by now in ruins.

A new governor was appointed in 1687, with orders to restore or replace the crumbling structure, but the defences were still incomplete in May 1690. By this time, France and England were once more at war, and Sir William Phips, with a militia contingent from Massachusetts, attacked, looted, and took possession of the town. The officials and residents were required to take an oath of loyalty to the English Crown, and although Phips and his men sailed away, Port Royal remained under English control, and a new French capital was established at Saint John. Hostilities continued, with French vessels raiding New England settlements and English forces retaliating.

English rule officially came to an end in 1697 with the Treaty of Ryswick, which restored Acadie to France. Port Royal once again became the capital, with Jacques-François de Monbeton de Brouillan appointed as commandant in 1701, and the town began to grow once more. With the re-establishment of government officials and a renewed garrison, both the civilian and military populations increased. Trade and industry expanded and social life flourished, particularly among the gentry, who formed the upper ranks of the military and administration. Brouillan immediately initiated construction of a new, larger fort on the site of the previous forts.

The following year, the outbreak of the War of the Spanish Succession meant that European powers were once again in conflict. To strengthen Acadia's defences, French engineer Pierre-Paul de Labat arrived in Port Royal and took over the reconstruction of the fort. It would be a state-of-the art establishment. The plan was based on the up-to-date designs of the French military engineer Vauban, with four bastions and a battery commanding seaward approaches. It included barracks, residences for officials, a chapel, armoury, powder magazine, forge, bakery, and store-house. This major project would take years to complete.

The European war inevitably spread to North America, and Acadie again became caught up in it. In 1704 a party of New England militiamen blockaded Port Royal and raided nearby Acadian settlements, but left the town unharmed. In June 1707 Port Royal itself was attacked while the fort was still unfinished. Governor Daniel d'Auger de Subercase, who had replaced Brouillan, defended the town as best he could, with the help of Acadians and Mi'kmaq. After destroying many of the town's houses, the raiders eventually left. Work continued on the fort, but in August the New Englanders returned. Once again they were repelled, after burning some Acadian homes on the river, and Labat urgently resumed work on the fort.

For the next few years while Port Royal was rebuilding, it was under constant threat of attack. That attack finally came in October 1710, when a fleet of British and New England ships commanded by Francis Nicholson entered the basin. Troops were landed and the final siege of Port Royal began. Soldiers and civilians took refuge inside the unfinished fort. A heavy bombardment followed, and this time Subercase was unable to repel the attackers. After a week of destruction, terms of surrender were negotiated. On October 16 the formal transfer of the fort took place, and Subercase ceremonially handed its keys over to Nicholson. It remained in British hands from then onwards. The key now on display at Fort Anne is one of those that Nicholson received. It was taken to Boston, where it would remain in private hands until it was donated to the Massachusetts Historical Society's museum. Then in 1922 the society's vice-president brought the key to Fort Anne and presented it to the people of Canada.

The town was renamed Annapolis Royal in honour of the Queen. With the fall of its capital, Acadie resumed the name Nova Scotia. The British replaced most of the buildings in the fort, which became known as Fort Anne, but the earthworks remain much as they were when originally designed by Labat, and the old French powder magazine can still be seen by visitors to the national historic site.

~ 10 ~

Saint-Ovide de Brouillon plate

EARLY 1700S

Fortress of Louisbourg National Historic Site, Louisbourg

T HIS PLATE, MADE OF FRENCH FAIENCE (A TYPE OF GLAZED ceramic ware), bears the coat of arms of Joseph de Monbeton de Brouillan (nephew of Jacques-François), known as Saint-Ovide de Brouillan, the second governor of Île Royale (Cape Breton Island). It is part of a dinner service made in southern France in the style developed at Moustiers-Sainte-Marie, and brought to Louisbourg by Saint-Ovide. Amazingly, it has survived the journey from France, the two British attacks on Louisbourg—including the fortress's final fall in 1758—and the more than 250 years since then.

But what brought Saint-Ovide to Louisbourg?

The story begins in 1713, when the Treaty of Utrecht ceded Newfoundland and mainland Nova Scotia to the British while the French retained control of Île Royale, now Cape Breton Island, and Île Saint-Jean, now Prince Edward Island. The inhabitants of the French colony of Plaisance in western Newfoundland, who were mostly fishermen, were relocated to Île Royale, where they could continue to make their living from the lucrative Atlantic cod fishery. Saint-Ovide de Brouillon had served as king's lieutenant in Plaisance, known to the British as Placentia, so he was ordered to oversee the transfer and resettlement of its residents. Louisbourg, formerly a small fishing village known as Havre à l'Anglois, was selected from three potential sites as the capital of the colony. It was also to be the site of a major fortress built to protect French interests in the North Atlantic and the Gulf of St. Lawrence. Saint-Ovide was appointed king's lieutenant in Île Royale in 1714, and in 1716 he was made administrator of the colony under the governor, Philippe Pastour de Costebelle. Two years later he replaced Costebelle as governor.

Having lost Placentia and the mainland of Nova Scotia, the French were anxious to protect their remaining territory in New France. A significant fortification gradually took shape at Louisbourg, which became a major centre for the cod fishery as well as a strategic port for trading vessels crossing the ocean or sailing to and from the St. Lawrence. Its military strength was designed to protect both fisheries and trade and, most importantly, to guard the route to Quebec. French soldiers were brought in to man the new fortress, and French supply vessels brought many of the necessities of life.

Under Saint-Ovide's leadership, a walled town began to replace the huddle of fishermen's houses by the shore. Louisbourg was home to civilians as well as soldiers, and as the colony's administrative centre it was the residence of the governor and other officials. There were also fishermen, artisans and tradesmen, shopkeepers and tavern keepers, clergy and nuns. Beside the relocated colonists from Plaisance and some Acadians from the mainland who had settled there, many of Louisbourg's inhabitants, both military and civilian, were French, and brought with them the tastes and customs of contemporary France.

Upper-class French officials, as well as better-off merchants and businessmen, did their best to maintain the lifestyle to which they were accustomed, and which included imported wines and spirits, oil, spices, and other luxury items. In season, they had access to fresh food from their gardens as well as from Acadian farms in Nova Scotia. But winters are long in Louisbourg, and by the time spring brought back the supply ships to the settlement, many larders were bare. Whatever the rigours of daily existence for ordinary people, however, for the governor, his entourage, and wealthier citizens, the table setting, the manners, and as far as possible the food itself, mirrored those of French households of equivalent rank. Louisbourg society in the first half on the eighteenth century, in many ways, resembled that of France.

The governor's apartments at Louisbourg formed part of the range of buildings protected by the King's Bastion. Saint-Ovide brought to his residence the splendid dinner service of which this plate formed a part. His dining room was the scene of elegant dinner parties with fine food and wine, served in an appropriate fashion. Imported items enhanced meals for which locally grown ingredients were prepared according to French traditions and served on fine china, with linen tablecloths and napkins. This plate, embellished with Saint-Ovide's coat of arms, would have graced the governor's table as he entertained important guests, military officers, clergy, and high-ranking civilians. The aristocratic lifestyle it exemplifies contrasted with the daily existence of many of the working people and ordinary soldiers.

Saint-Ovide served as governor until 1739, for a major portion of Louisbourg's existence. During his early years in office he was successful in establishing the fortress and town in unpromising surroundings, but his work was marred by disputes with many of his officials, and later in his administration his personal commercial interests frequently conflicted with his official responsibilities. When he was replaced as governor, he returned to France and sold most of his property on Île Royale. His dinner service, however, remained at Louisbourg and may have been used by his successors.

Louisbourg continued to grow until 1745, when for the first time it fell to a British force consisting largely of New Englanders. For a few years the fortress remained under British control, until the Treaty of Aix-la-Chapelle returned it to France in 1748. Ten years later, it fell to the British for the second time, and its defences were destroyed.

Louisbourg lay in ruins and partially buried for nearly two centuries, and some of its building stone was taken for use as far away as Halifax. It would not be until the early 1920s that many of its buildings would be uncovered and partially restored by the federal government. Today, all classes of Louisbourg society are represented in the partial reconstruction of the fortress. Visitors can even view some of the items that survived its siege and fall, including Saint-Ovide de Brouillon's plate. Even now, archaeologists continue to discover items that tell the story of this remote French settlement that played such a major role in our province's history.

~11~

Domestic iron cauldron

PRE-1755

Grand Pré National Historic Site

T HIS BIG, THREE-LEGGED IRON COOKING POT WAS AN ESSENTIAL
item in a mid-eighteenth-century Acadian home in the village
of Grand Pré. Cauldrons like this were used to prepare soups
and stews on the open fireplace, using the meat of animals raised on
the family farm, fish caught in the Gaspereau River or the nearby Minas
Basin, or game brought home from a hunting expedition. Vegetables and

herbs for seasoning came from the kitchen garden beside the house, and the aroma from the simmering pot would often fill the family room that formed the ground floor of an Acadian house. But this particular cauldron had a second, more unusual career: as the guardian of buried treasure.

Acadian families began to settle in Grand Pré around 1680, when Pierre Melanson arrived with his wife, Marie Mius d'Entremont, and their children. They were joined soon afterwards by Pierre Terriot and his wife, Cécile Landry. Other families arrived, and together they worked to drain the salt marshes of Grand Pré by building dykes to hold back the high Fundy tides. Through this process, they created pastures and fertile fields where wheat and other crops were grown. Acadian farming settlements soon grew up on marshlands all around the Minas Basin. Their livelihood was based on farming, and they sold their surplus produce to the citizens of Port Royal and to New England merchants. In turn, the Acadians purchased manufactured goods, frequently from these same merchants. This cauldron may have been among the items acquired by an Acadian family with the profits from their trade. But what is its significance?

This cauldron is not just an Acadian housewife's kitchen equipment. It was put to quite a different use at a crucial point in Nova Scotia's history. The seventeenth and early eighteenth centuries were turbulent times in Europe, and in European colonies in North America. Wars between England and France spread across the Atlantic, where they often focused on the control of Acadie, or as the English called it, Nova Scotia. The colony had officially changed hands several times before the Melansons and the Terriots came to Grand Pré. In 1713 British possession was finally established by the terms of the Treaty of Utrecht, which left the French-speaking Catholic population subject to English Protestant rule, creating an uneasy situation for both sides.

At this time, the population of Grand Pré formed the largest Acadian settlement in Nova Scotia. Officially neutral, in 1730 its members had reluctantly signed an oath of allegiance to the British crown. They did so, however, on condition that they would not be required to take up arms against the French or the Mi'kmaq, who had been their allies since the early days of settlement. Even after signing the oath, the Acadians were still regarded with suspicion by the British administration—particularly after 1749, when Halifax was established as the capital of Nova Scotia, and efforts were renewed to have them sign an unconditional oath of allegiance. Most Acadians were unwilling to do so.

Meanwhile, disagreement had arisen between Britain and France about the location of the Acadie/Nova Scotia border that had been agreed to in 1713. The dispute escalated, and French troops established a fort at Beauséjour on the Chignecto Isthmus in support of French claims. With the threat of war looming, British authorities feared that in the event of an invasion, the Acadians and the Mi'kmaq would support the French—as some of them undoubtedly would. The matter of the oath became more urgent, and when the demands were again met with refusal, Governor Charles Lawrence determined that the Acadians should be deported.

In September 1755, troops under the command of Lieutenant-Colonel John Winslow rounded up the men and boys of Grand Pré in their church, Saint-Charles-des-Mines, where Winslow announced the plans for deportation. He held the men prisoner until they were taken to the ships that would transport the entire Acadian community to Britain's American colonies to the south. They remained on board, waiting for their wives and children to join them. On October 8, the remainder of Grand Pré's population was forced to embark. In the confusion, not all families were reunited as promised. The captive Acadians waited on the ships until the end of the month, while Acadians from the more distant villages were rounded up and brought to join them. Finally, the fleet set sail. Its passengers would be scattered along the American east coast to Massachusetts, Connecticut, Pennsylvania, Maryland, and Virginia.

While the women and children awaited their fate, they made provision for their involuntary voyage. They were allowed to take with them only a few essentials, which meant that many possessions had to be left behind. Most objects would be destroyed or seized by Winslow's soldiers once their owners were aboard the ships. But some treasures, it seems, were buried to keep them from English hands, and with the hope that someday their owners might return and retrieve them.

This cauldron was dug up in a farmer's field in Grand Pré in the 1920s, after lying hidden for 170 years. Concealed inside was a smaller, earthenware pot, filled with moss and bark to protect the fragile objects it contained: a pair of glass cruets (small, narrow-necked bottles) and their glazed and decorated earthenware stand, which have survived with very little damage. The stand is of the type known as tinware, because of its opaque white tin-oxide glaze. Oral tradition has identified the glass vessels as having been used in the celebration of mass. It is also possible that they were designed for domestic use, but the fact that they were so carefully buried suggests a serious effort to keep sacred religious objects out of the hands of British Protestant heretics. In this, their keepers were certainly successful. The iron pot and its contents are among the few precious objects that have survived in Nova Scotia from the days before the Deportation.

~ 12 ~

Zwicker Bible

1736

Mahone Bay Settlers Museum

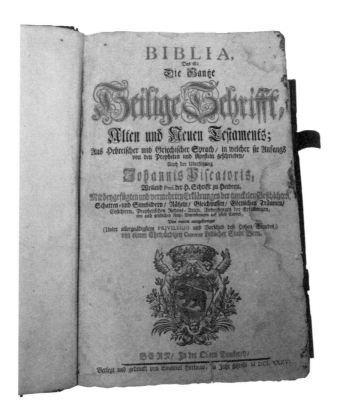

I MAGINE CROSSING THE ATLANTIC IN AN EIGHTEENTH-CENTURY
sailing ship, on a voyage that could last between two and three
months, to a place about which you knew nothing. A cramped space,

about two metres square, was allocated to four passengers, with their meagre baggage allowance stowed under the bunks. Food and water were limited. It was under these conditions that shiploads of so-called Foreign Protestants left Europe—and most of their worldly possessions—for Nova Scotia in the early 1750s. They brought with them only the most essential items of clothing and personal property.

In 1749, soon after Halifax was established, Nova Scotia's governor, Edward Cornwallis, had asked the British government to send Protestant settlers to counterbalance the region's Acadian Catholic population. British citizens proved reluctant to leave home, so an agent was sent to recruit Protestant families from parts of Germany, France, and Switzerland, where they formed a minority. They were promised land and rations while they got themselves established but were responsible for the expense of their voyage. Twelve shiploads of these Foreign Protestants arrived in Halifax between 1750 and 1752.

Peter Zwicker and his family were among those who had been recruited from Germany's Palatinate territory. Peter was a thirty-six-year-old farmer from Zeiskam, near Landau. He brought with him his wife, Maria Magdalena, and their five children: Peter, the eldest, aged sixteen, two more boys, and two girls. The family sailed from Rotterdam in 1752 on board the *Gale*, destined for Halifax. Pious Calvinists, their essentials included this Bible. The massive leather-bound book with decorative brass corners, a brass stud on the cover, and a clasp, would have occupied a good deal of the family's allotted space. Its title page, printed in red and black, mostly in the old German black-letter type, tells us it is a German translation by the Calvinist theologian Johannes Piscator, printed in Bern in 1736. This was an expensive book, made to last, with good rag paper and a sturdy leather binding, and was clearly a well-cared-for family treasure.

The *Gale* docked on September 6, 1752, in Halifax, where her passengers joined other German, French, and Swiss immigrants—some of whom had arrived two years earlier and were still waiting to be settled on their promised land. They found temporary quarters in Halifax, where they spent the winter. After this inauspicious beginning, the following year they were once again put onto a ship, and transferred to the new settlement of Lunenburg at the head of a bay on Nova Scotia's South Shore. The newcomers initially lived within the town boundaries for security, but gradually scattered farther afield.

As well as his town lot on Fox Street in Lunenburg, Peter Zwicker received a thirty-acre farm lot on the southwest side of Mahone Bay. Here, the Zwickers became one of the village's founding families. They built what was said to be the first house on that side of the water, where the Bible would have been read daily. After a good life in their new country, Maria Magdalena died in Mahone Bay in 1787, followed by Peter in 1789.

Peter Jr. was married in 1759 and lived on the homestead with his bride, Anna Catherina Schmid (or Smith). His sister, Maria Magdalena, had married Philip Hayson (or Heison), whose family owned the adjoining lot, two months earlier. Soon after his marriage, Peter Jr. purchased a farm lot at Oakland, and another east of there, in partnership with his brother-in-law, Philip. He also acquired a farm lot on the Northwest Range. In addition, in 1764 he drew one of the three hundred-acre forest lots in the Third Division on Little Mushamush Lake. By the time he came to make his will in 1811, Peter Zwicker Jr. had clearly prospered, as he also owned land at Blockhouse, Clearland, and Indian Point, and a sawmill. On his death in 1813, the land was left among his surviving nine sons (by two marriages), and £500 were to be divided among his seven daughters, along with "1 cow, 2 sheep, and a complete new feather bed." The Reform (Calvinist) Church in Lunenburg, where the Zwickers worshipped, was to receive £25. Peter Jr. was well educated; he was known as "Doctor," and in his will he left a collection of books "to be sold at public auction among his own family to defray funeral expenses." Whether the Bible was included in the sale is not made clear, but in any case, it was carefully preserved after Peter's death and remained in the family until it was donated to the Mahone Bay Settlers Museum.

Descendants of Peter Zwicker remained in Mahone Bay, and by 1818 were running the old Zwicker home as an inn. It was here that Lady Dalhousie, the wife of the lieutenant-governor, spent a happy vacation with their children and her entourage in the summer of 1818, while his lordship undertook expeditions to other settlements. The Zwicker Inn's reputation for hospitality has survived, as the name has been reused by more recent Mahone Bay restaurants.

Religion was important to the German families in Lunenburg County, both Calvinist and Lutheran, and German Bibles from both traditions survive. The settlers retained their language, particularly for religious worship, for several generations. The custom of preaching in German, and the use of German Bibles, hymnals, and sermon collections in private homes maintained the language in the area well into the nineteenth century. In the peaceful old cemetery at Mahone Bay are the graves of Maria Magdalena Zwicker and Peter Zwicker *der Erste* ("the first"). Created by a skilled craftsman, the inscriptions on their gravestones appear in German, in the same old-style lettering as the printed pages of their family Bible. An earlier stone, commemorating Anna Catharina Zwicker, wife of Peter the second, who died on October 27, 1780, is more primitive. All three begin with the traditional words, *Hier ruhet in Gott*, meaning "Here rests in God." May they continue to do so.

～ 13 ～

Captain William Bishop's sword

PRE-1781

Kings County Museum, Kentville

M Y GUIDE AT THE KINGS COUNTY MUSEUM PROUDLY pointed out this officer's sword, with its ornamental hilt and finely decorated blade, now mounted with its scabbard in a display case on the wall. The date assigned to it, 1781, is that of the so-called Battle of Blomidon, in which its owner, Captain William Bishop, may have used it. It is part of the much longer story of the Bishop family.

The Bishops came to Horton Township from New London, Connecticut, in 1760. They were among the New Englanders known as Planters, who responded to Governor Lawrence's call for settlers to work the vacant Acadian farmlands. The head of the household was John Bishop, whose father, Eleazar, had emigrated from England to Connecticut in the early 1690s. John was fifty-one when he came to Nova Scotia with Hannah, his second wife. Their four sons—John Jr., twenty-nine, William, twenty-eight, Peter, twenty-five and Timothy, twenty—were already grown up.

Before coming to Nova Scotia, John Jr. and William had both served in the Seven Years' War (1754–1763), during which Britain and France struggled for control of territory in North America. William, a captain in the 3rd Connecticut Militia Regiment, was stationed at Fort Edward on the Hudson River in 1756. The following year, he was made a sergeant in Captain John Latimore's Company, which was called upon to relieve the besieged British troops at Fort William Henry. Having avoided the slaughter that followed British surrender, Sergeant William Bishop returned home to Connecticut, where, within a few years, his father decided to accept Governor Charles Lawrence's offer of land in Nova Scotia. By that time, William had been promoted to the rank of captain, and, as an officer, carried this sword.

The Bishops were among the more well-to-do New England Planters who arrived at Horton Landing with their compatriots in 1760, bringing with them supplies and stock in preparation for establishing a farm. After being granted land that had been developed by the Acadians at Greenwich in Horton Township, the Bishop family was soon working the farmland that would be handed down through generations of Bishops and is now known as Noggins Corner.

William Bishop's peaceful agricultural life in Nova Scotia was interrupted, however, by the American Revolutionary War. Action was not confined to the New England mainland. American privateering vessels sailed along Nova Scotia's Atlantic coast and into the Bay of Fundy and the Minas Basin, seizing ships and looting property. Local militia companies were formed in many rural communities to defend their citizens against these raids. The Townships of Horton and Cornwallis together mustered some one hundred men, including William.

Militia companies were composed of residents who had regular occupations, and when, on May 21, 1781, a marauding American vessel rounded Cape Blomidon into the Minas Basin it took the busy inhabitants by surprise. Amos Sheffield, a Cornwallis merchant, was preparing his ship to leave with a cargo bound for Saint John when the raiders descended and seized it. Despite Sheffield's efforts at resistance, assisted by William Bishop and his companions, the privateers took them prisoner and prepared to sail away with the schooner and their captives.

Fortunately for Sheffield and his men, Benjamin Belcher witnessed the raid and rode quickly over to Horton, where he mustered twenty-eight militiamen and a schooner, and set off in pursuit. They caught up with the privateers, who were slowed down by the Minas Basin's strong incoming tide as they were attempting to leave. The skirmish that ensued is known as the Battle of Blomidon. Belcher and his men recovered the stolen vessel and freed the captives; they then took part in the fight, which ended in the capture of three enemy ships.

Watson Kirkconnell, former president of Acadia University, has immortalized this event in his poem "The Battle of Blomidon," which closes with these lines:

> *And promptly Will Bishop and Jonathan Crane*
> *Discomfit their guards and a victory gain.*
> *Thus over the Basin by noon we withdrew*
> *With three captured ships and our jubilant crew.*
> *"The blow that we struck at the Cape was a squelcher!"*
> *Remarked our stout commodore, Benjamin Belcher.*

This battle seems to have been the last military action seen by Captain William Bishop. He returned to his farm and continued to manage it until he died in Horton in 1815.

A number of John Bishop's descendants have continued to live and farm in the area to this day, but not all succeeding generations stayed in Nova Scotia, and neither did the sword. The records of the Bishop Family Association trace the sword's ownership through William's descendants, showing that it probably passed by way of his son, William Dennison Bishop, to his grandson, Gurdon, and great-grandson, Adolphus, who inherited the sword in 1875. Adolphus Bishop lived in New Minas, then in Canaan and Grand Pré, but his son, Charles A. Bishop, the next owner, moved away to the United States. He became a judge in Sycamore, Illinois, where it is said he kept the sword on a closet shelf. After the death of Charles's widow in 1946, the sword went to their son Stuart Bishop, in

Indianapolis, who died in 1955. When Stuart's wife died in 1960, the sword became the property of their daughter, Patricia (Bishop) Gutting, and her husband, Paul, who lived in Elm Grove, Wisconsin. Patricia renewed her link to Nova Scotia when the couple attended the first Bishop family reunion in Wolfville in 1982. It was their son, Jeffrey, who decided that after its long journey, the sword should return to "its rightful place" in Nova Scotia.

In August 2004, on the occasion of the annual Bishop family gathering, an American family member presented the sword on the Guttings' behalf to the Bishop Family Association. Later that year, the association presented the much-travelled weapon to the Kings County Museum, where it remains one of its treasures.

❦ 14 ❦

Singing school music book

1766

Colchester Historical Museum and Archives, Truro

THIS COLOURFUL PAGE COMES FROM A HANDWRITTEN, HAND-made book in the collection of the Colchester Historical Museum and Archives. It contains musical notation for thirteen psalm tunes and is decorated with brightly coloured, primitive illustrations. Both ownership and authorship are identified by the title words "MARY MILLER HER BOOK *per me* (by me) John McClorg 1766." It changed hands several times, for inside the front cover other names appear: "Samuel Miller Halifax"; "John Densmore his Book"; and "Mary Elsie Densmore's Book 1912 12 years old." On the flyleaf is written, in somewhat shaky Latin, *Ego vide Lex et Rex Johannes McClorg*, above a pen drawing of a bird. A brief introduction with a chart introduces the "fasola" musical notation used in the book: "For to attain the Skill of Musick and Learn Gamut up and down by heart thereby to Know your rules and spaces notes."

Thirteen tunes follow, identified by name. Each is written on a conventional staff of five lines but uses only the four notes fa, so, la, and mi, represented by their initials. The pages are decorated with drawings of a variety of subjects, including a bare-breasted mermaid, a unicorn with forelegs and a fish's tail, a peacock, a vase of flowers, a woman with a teapot and cups, and Adam and Eve in the Garden of Eden (the only Biblical theme). The page shown here illustrates the proverb "A bird in the hand is worth two in the bush," and decorates the tune "Marys," intriguingly identified as "the ale wifs Pater Noster." At the back of the book are a few lines added by Samuel Miller, Mary's brother, dated 1782: "Unto the Lord Every Knee shall Bow to the most High All Tongues Bless Before God Every Mouth is stopt And all the World is become [—] before the Lord of Hosts."

Books like this originated in schools established by singing masters to train lay people to read simple church music. According to music historian Nancy Vogan, singing masters usually held these schools two or three evenings a week for three or four months during fall and winter. The course culminated in a presentation under the direction of the singing master. These schools were found among Protestant congregations in both Old and New Worlds. It is said that they were popular because young women were not required to be chaperoned while attending them, as they were on many social occasions.

The manuscript music books included the tunes of the most popular metrical psalms. Although some printed versions are known, many singing masters custom-made books for their students, including the students' personal choice of tunes and resulting in some variety of content. In some similar books, each note was identified using a different shape, giving rise to the term "shape-note music."

This book gives a tantalizing glimpse of the original owner, Mary Miller, who came to the Truro area in 1769 with her parents, William and Ann Miller, and her brothers, William and Samuel. The family arrived that year on board the *Admiral Hawke* as part of a group of over one hundred Presbyterians of Scottish descent from Londonderry, Ireland. Alexander McNutt, a land agent who had previously brought Scots-Irish Planters to the Cobequid Bay area from New Hampshire in the early 1760s, recruited the family to work on an Acadian farm. Among the possessions that Mary brought with her was this book, dated three years before her emigration to Nova Scotia. According to the museum, Mary, at the age of nineteen, had attended one of the singing schools back in Londonderry, along with her friends. The book is a record of the tunes that they sang, and the method by which they learned them. The knowledge was clearly important to Mary, as she brought it with her to her new home. But we know nothing of her life here.

We know a little more about John McClorg, compiler of the book. At the time it was made, he lived at Templemoyle in Londonderry and was master of the singing school Mary Miller attended. Hers was not the only book he made. An account of the McClurgs (a variant spelling) of Templemoyle states that: "A manuscript book of Psalm Tunes etc. has survived given to David McClorg in 1766 by his brother John McClorg who later emigrated to America along with three other brothers in the second half of the 18th century." David, who probably attended his brother's classes at about the same time as Mary, remained at Templemoyle, while John and his other brothers settled in Pennsylvania. Did John perhaps continue to organize singing schools among his fellow Ulstermen and make more books? It seems likely. There is a 1776 record of a John McClorg and his family as members of the Guinston Presbyterian Church in Chanceford Township, Pennsylvania, where we may imagine that the congregation benefitted from his instruction.

Mary Miller's book seems to have passed to her brother Samuel, but

what became of it after Samuel's death? How did it come into the possession of John and Elizabeth Densmore? The only link I have found
between the families is a record of the marriage of a John C. Densmore,
aged forty-three, to a Mabel Grace Miller, aged thirty-five, in 1907 at
Noel Shore. Although over one hundred years of the book's history are
missing, it remains a valuable example of the link between the eighteenth-
century immigrants and their homeland, reflecting a musical and religious
tradition that spanned the Atlantic at that time.

～ 15 ～

Fire pumper, Friendly Fire Club

1750

Shelburne County Museum, Shelburne

SHELBURNE COUNTY MUSEUM STAFF MEMBERS WERE UNANIMOUS in recommending this ancient fire pumper, dating back to the early years of Loyalist settlement, as the most significant object in their collection. In the early twentieth century this wooden fire engine could be seen on the lawn in front of a Shelburne house, where it was being used as a planter. It had begun to rot away, but was rescued from this fate on behalf of the museum. It has since been restored by a conservator, and now has place of pride in the museum's collection.

The first four hundred families who arrived in Shelburne in 1783 after the American Revolutionary War came mostly from New York. They were known as the Port Roseway Associates, from the French name for the harbour, Port Razoir. In order to remain British subjects, they had opted to take up Governor Parr's offer of free land in Nova Scotia, with government support for the initial settlement period. They were soon joined by further waves of Loyalists, and by 1784 Shelburne's population had swollen to around ten thousand (athough many of these people soon moved to other parts of Nova Scotia).

The newly arrived Loyalists were accustomed to running their civic affairs in an orderly fashion, and one of the first things they did after arriving at Port Roseway was to establish a fire company, called the Friendly Fire Club. A copy of *Rules and Orders Formed for the Regulation of the Members of the Friendly Fire Club, Instituted at Shelburne, the Fifth day of August, 1784*, the Fire Club's membership booklet, has also survived. Its original owner was Henry Guest, whose name, and the date 1785, is inscribed on the inside front cover. The booklet contains the club's original ten rules, with additional rules handwritten on some blank pages, and a list of the twenty-eight founding members, including Guest. Some of these names are crossed out, probably because the members in question moved away, though two are noted as "deceased." Also included is an additional handwritten list of men who joined the club after 1784. A facsimile edition of the booklet was published in 1982, with additional biographical notes by Shelburne historian Mary Archibald, giving information about the people mentioned. Henry Guest, we learn, was a jeweller who served as one of the town's twelve fire wards.

The houses and business premises of Shelburne, like those elsewhere in Nova Scotia, were made of wood. Fire was a constant hazard, as open fires were used for cooking and heating and chimneys were not always well constructed. There was no shortage of water, but it had to be delivered to the site of the conflagration. Shelburne's volunteer firefighters originally formed a bucket brigade, referred to in the club's second rule, which states:

> That each member shall provide himself with Two Bags, sufficient to contain Three Bushels each, with proper Strings for the greater Dispatch in closing the same; to be marked with the Owner's Christian Name and Sirname [sic] at length: likewise Two Buckets and a Hat, with a round black Brim, and a Crown painted white, and having F. F. C. marked as large as the Front of the Crown will admit; all these to be kept constantly hanging in the most convenient part of his House, and never to be removed or used, except in Case of Fire, under Penalty of Twenty Shillings.

It soon became apparent that this bags-and-buckets system did not meet the needs of the growing town. In 1785 James Robertson and Benjamin Davis bought two mobile pumping machines, forerunners of our modern fire trucks, at a cost of £57 on behalf of the newly formed Shelburne Chamber of Commerce, for the use of the members of the Friendly Fire Club. Machines of this type had been used in New York since the 1730s, so the people of Shelburne were familiar with them. The two pumpers, however, were not new; they had been made around 1750 by the English manufacturer Richard Newsham, who took out patents for his invention in the early 1720s in both England and North America, where they quickly became popular.

One of the two pumpers purchased by the Club has since vanished, but the one featured here somehow survived, and is thought to be among the oldest of its kind in North America. The body consists of a tank, which would presumably have been filled at all times in case of an urgent summons to a fire. Once at the site of the conflagration, the tank could be topped up by a bucket brigade. The pumping mechanism was operated by men on either side who raised and lowered the horizontal bars alternately, forcing the water through a cylinder by means of a piston, and creating a jet of water that could be directed onto the blaze with a leather hose. This was hard labour, but it seems to have been effective, as these early fire engines served the citizens of Shelburne for many years before being retired.

For a long time, it was believed that King George III had given the pumper to the town of Shelburne in recognition of the settlers' loyalty to the British Crown: decorative ceramics portraying the machine identify it as a royal gift. But documents found in the Shelburne Court House in the 1980s record the details of the citizens' purchase of two fire pumpers, and their delivery from London. Despite the shattering of the more romantic story, the antiquity and provenance of these items was established, and this surviving example is an invaluable artefact that connects modern museum-goers to Shelburne's earliest days.

～ 16 ～
Loyalist candle mould

1780s
Jost Heritage House, Sydney

O N A STREET IN A QUIET RESIDENTIAL AREA OF SYDNEY, Nova Scotia, stands one of the earliest buildings to be constructed in the town. Originally the home of merchant and shipowner Samuel Sparrow, it is now open to the public as a museum, housing artefacts that represent significant periods in its history, including this candle mould.

Cape Breton Island has a varied history. The last military stronghold of the French, until the fall of Louisbourg in 1758, it remained a remote and neglected part of Nova Scotia until it was brought to life again by the influx of Loyalists in the 1780s. In 1785 it became a separate British colony, with the expectation that Loyalists looking for land and opportunity would come to develop its resources. The settlement of Sydney, at the head of Spanish Bay, was established as its capital that same year. The newly appointed governor, Joseph Frederick Wallet DesBarres, laid out his new town in a pattern of streets that can still be seen today.

The Jost House, built in 1786 to serve as a home for the Sparrow family, takes its name from a later owner. In Samuel Sparrow's time, it was a one-and-a-half-storey house with a gable roof and dormer windows at the front. The kitchen, with its heavy beamed ceiling, was in the basement. The open fireplace was used for cooking, with pots suspended from an iron hook over the flames. Built into the wall to the left of the fireplace is a "beehive" bake oven with a curved brick top, of the kind commonly used in the New England homes from which the settlers had come. For baking, a separate fire was built in the oven, and when the masonry had reached the required temperature, the ashes were swept out and the risen dough placed inside.

The kitchen has since been restored and maintained as it would have been when the Sparrows occupied the house. Other items on view represent the everyday objects essential to domestic life in the eighteenth century. Some of them—things like ladles and strainers—are similar to those we use today. Others remind us of an era when women's work was much different: cooking and cleaning were done without the help of modern appliances, and plastic was unknown; there were no frozen or canned foods, and everything was prepared from scratch in home kitchens, using wooden spoons and wooden or ceramic mixing bowls. Most of the items used in eighteenth-century households have their counterparts—electric-powered, better-designed, or plastic-made—in modern kitchens, but a few have become obsolete. Among the treasures in the basement kitchen of Jost House is an item that was once essential: a candle mould for domestic candle making.

With no electricity, homes were lit by candles when darkness fell. Domestic candles for ordinary household use were frequently homemade with tallow, derived from animal fat, or wax made from spermaceti or whale oil, by-products of the whaling industry. Since they were the chief source of artificial light, many candles were needed on dark winter evenings, and a constant supply had to be maintained. Candle moulds like this one, made of metal, were designed for making candles in batches of twelve (one piece is missing from this example). The candles were made by pouring melted wax or tallow into moulds after wicks had been inserted. Wicks were made from twisted strands of cotton, which were threaded through the holes at the top and secured at the other end. The mould was then inverted and the wax or tallow poured in. When cooled, the candles could be lifted out. Moulds like this would have been in regular use in the Sparrow household, and in other early Sydney homes, throughout much of the nineteenth century, until commercially made candles replaced them.

Samuel Sparrow lived in Sydney for only two years before leaving for London and then South Carolina, where he died around 1800. Cape Breton did not remain a separate colony for long afterwards. It was re-annexed to Nova Scotia in 1802, and instead of developing as a colonial capital the settlement became an industrial town based around the coal-mining industry. The family of Thomas Jost, a merchant from Halifax, occupied the present house for many years. After purchasing the property in 1836, Jost made a considerable number of alterations: the house now has two full storeys, though portions of the original building are intact. The ground floor included in the front room, from which Jost operated a store, as well as a parlour, dining room, and bedroom, and the upper floor was enlarged. In the 1850s Jost built a new store beside the original house, which was kept as the family residence. His descendants lived there until 1971. The basement kitchen remained in use until the late 1800s.

Now restored to its original state, and furnished with period items like this candle mould, the room and its contents, along with the rest of the house, operate as a museum, reflecting the domestic life of the Sparrows and other pioneer settlers in the Cape Breton colony.

~ 17 ~

Black Loyalist pearlware dish

PRE-1783

Black Loyalist Historical Museum, Birchtown

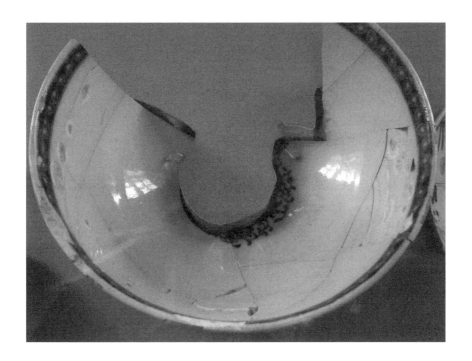

IN THE EIGHTEENTH CENTURY MANY WELL-TO-DO AMERICAN
families kept Black slaves. The slave trade was, at that time, a lucrative
business for those engaged in bringing shiploads of West African na-
tives to North America, under deplorable conditions, as source of cheap
agricultural and domestic labour. While some former slaves managed to

buy their freedom during the American Revolutionary War (1775–1783), the majority of Blacks were still considered the chattels of their white owners and subject to appalling punishment if they tried to escape. In order to increase their manpower during the American Revolutionary War, the British government offered freedom to those Blacks who agreed to enlist with or support the Loyalists. Many Blacks took advantage of this opportunity, and, in the aftermath of the revolution, a contingent of freed Blacks joined the Loyalist migration to Nova Scotia beginning in 1783. This dish is among the remnants of the Black Loyalists' sojourn here.

While the town on the east side of Shelburne's harbour was being laid out for the white immigrants, the newly emancipated Blacks were given land on a bay to the northwest. The Blacks named their settlement Birchtown in honour of New York governor Brigadier-General Samuel Birch, who had given many of them their certificates of freedom. Among the new arrivals were Colonel Stephen Blucke and his wife, Margaret. Blucke, the son of a white father and a black mother, had been born free in Barbados and was well educated, as was Margaret, who came from New York, where many members of her family were free and well-to-do. Like them, she had been able to buy her freedom. She also secured the emancipation of a young black girl, Isabella Gibbons, who accompanied the Bluckes to Nova Scotia and was then adopted into their family. Educated and accustomed to freedom, the Bluckes became the leaders of the new community. Stephen Blucke had commanded a military unit in New Jersey during the war, and organized a Black Militia when he came to Birchtown. He served as magistrate, supervised the Black Militia's employment in public works, including road construction, and also built one of Birchtown's first fishing boats. He was appointed schoolmaster of the community's one-room schoolhouse in 1785.

Some 2,500 people were living in Birchtown by 1784, making it the largest North American settlement of free Blacks. Though they had arrived with high expectations of being treated equally to the white settlers, the Black Loyalists were to be disappointed. While they were no longer slaves, the Blacks of Birchtown were still considered second-class citizens.

Lacking education, they had few opportunities for work, other than as domestics or unskilled labourers for the citizens of Shelburne, across the harbour. Their wages were so low that white workers protested because they could not compete in the labour market. Their violent protest is known today as the Shelburne Riots.

While the Bluckes were able to build a substantial home, the majority of Birchtown's population was marginalized and impoverished. The Black Loyalists had particular difficulty growing sufficient food for their families on their rocky, unproductive land, so when government rations expired, many suffered extreme hunger. In 1787 the Black Loyalists were eventually granted farm lots some kilometres from the main community, but the poor soil of this region did not offer much hope of improvement. Without the means to build permanent dwellings, some continued to live for several years in pit houses, the small, sunken huts roofed with roughly hewn tree branches and moss that had first sheltered them on their arrival.

Far from the prosperity and equality that they had expected freedom to bring, and in spite of Blucke's leadership, the Birchtown community, poor and disillusioned, barely survived. Nova Scotia had not lived up to the Black Loyalists' expectations, and the white inhabitants of Shelburne (many of whom had also failed to achieve the comfort they were accustomed to) did not accept them. Their chief consolation was religion. Birchtown settlers were mainly Methodists, Baptists, and Anglicans, though the Bluckes were the only family prosperous enough to afford a pew in Shelburne's Anglican church. The rest of the population heard preachers such as Moses Wilkinson at his Methodist meeting house in Birchtown, and David George, who established a Baptist church at Blacktown, between Birchtown and Shelburne.

Meanwhile, there were also impoverished and discontented Blacks, both freed slaves and Loyalists, living in England. In 1788 Granville Sharp formed the Sierra Leone Company with the aim of creating a new colony of free Blacks in West Africa, the home of their ancestors. In 1790 Thomas Peters, a freed slave representing Blacks in Nova Scotia, travelled to England to meet with abolitionists, including Granville Sharp, and indicated interest in joining Sharp's proposed colony. Sharp sent John Clarkson to Nova Scotia to recruit those who wished to leave and found many who were anxious to seize the opportunity. They included the majority of the Birchtown settlers, who left in 1792.

Stephen Blucke opposed the move and did not go with them. His leadership had clearly diminished. His wife had left him four years earlier, and he continued to live with Isabella Gibbons, with whom he had a daughter. He was accused of theft, left the community, and disappeared from history. The population of Birchtown dwindled, and eventually the remaining Black Loyalists scattered.

In 1998 a team of archaeologists discovered this elegant blue-and-white pearlware dish at the site thought to be the Blucke home. A fine, glazed white ceramic material, often, as in this case, decorated with a blue motif, pearlware was popularized by Josiah Wedgwood in 1779, and was very fashionable at the time of the American Revolutionary War. Despite the hardship surrounding the community, the artefacts found on the house-site suggest a comfortable lifestyle. This dish is now displayed at the Black Loyalist Historical Museum, where the Black Loyalist Heritage Society preserves the memory of Birchtown, and the few artefacts remaining from the settlement.

～ 18 ～

Quaker House shoes

PRE-1785

Quaker House, Dartmouth

HOW DID THESE TATTERED OLD SHOES COME TO BE ON DISPLAY in a downtown Dartmouth house?

Although outlawed today, the hunting and killing of whales was an important part of the eighteenth- and nineteenth-century economy on the east coast of North America and continued well into the twentieth. The Quaker House (1786), operated since 1971 as part of the Dartmouth Heritage Museum, is a survivor from the short-lived period, between 1785 and 1795, when whaling was a major industry in this community. Before the invention of kerosene in the nineteenth century, the oil obtained from whale blubber was widely used in lamps. It was also used in the manufacture of soap and margarine, as a lubricant, and for other industrial purposes for many years. The wax known as spermaceti, obtained from the head cavity of the sperm whale, was particularly valuable in the manufacture of candles and cosmetics.

Whaling was a dirty and dangerous activity. Ships travelled long distances and sometimes spent years at sea, leaving the crews' wives to take care of domestic affairs. But when it was successful, whaling was a very lucrative business—both for the owners of the vessels and for the crew, who shared in the profits. It provided a living not only for the men who went to sea, but also for the workers in the processing plants, and for those who serviced the whaling fleet and produced equipment for the industry.

The island of Nantucket in Massachusetts was home to a major whaling fleet before the Revolutionary War. Threatened by the wartime destruction of many of these vessels and Britain's imposition of a tax on American whale oil, a group of Nantucket whalers made a life-changing decision to move their operation to Dartmouth in 1785. Like many other Nantucket residents, these people were Quakers: hardworking, honest, and good businessmen. They built wharves, warehouses, and processing facilities in Dartmouth, including two spermaceti-candle factories. They also set up workshops to produce the equipment needed to support their industry. And finally, they built houses for themselves, including the one on Ochterloney Street in which the shoes were found.

Now a museum, the Quaker House was once the home of cooper William Ray, whose job was to make the barrels in which whale oil was stored. He lived here with his family for ten years, in what is now considered the oldest house in Dartmouth. The architectural style of William Ray's house resembles typical Nantucket Quaker houses: solidly built, with an off-centre front door, large, light rooms, and a huge central chimney. During restoration work on the house, workers found that the beams used in its construction were all numbered. This suggests that the Ray house in Nantucket may have been dismantled and brought to Dartmouth to be reassembled on arrival. But there would be another, even more fascinating discovery inside Quaker House.

While the restorations were being carried out in 1971, these much-worn shoes were found between the inner and outer planking of the walls. They are not a pair, but two of four individual shoes that were hidden in the walls of the house when it was originally constructed. The pious Dartmouth Quakers were not immune to old superstitions. It was thought that if you put one half of a pair of shoes into the wall of your home, the devil would be so busy looking for the other shoe that he wouldn't bother you. Hiding several shoes seems to have provided extra insurance, so William Ray had these shoes and two others embedded in the walls of his house. Thus protected, he lived there peacefully and carried on his trade. Today, these shoes are among the many interesting items on display in the Quaker House Museum that tell the story of the Quakers who worked in Dartmouth's short-lived whaling industry.

The Quaker whalers did not remain long in Dartmouth, though their business there was prospering. They were in fact so successful that they were seen as competition for whaling companies in other parts of the world. As a result, after only ten years in Dartmouth, they were enticed to transfer their whaling operations to Milford Haven in Wales, where Britain's economy—and the tax collector—would benefit from their industry. A few individuals remained in Dartmouth, but the glory days of its whaling industry were over.

Most of the houses built by the whaling community have long since vanished, but for some reason William Ray's home has survived. Perhaps credit is due to the protection of the shoes once embedded within its walls.

～ 19 ～

Whale's tooth with scrimshaw decoration

1800

Queens County Museum, Liverpool

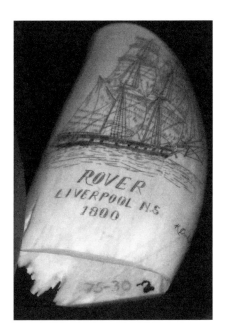

HAT DID CREW MEMBERS OF THE SAILING SHIPS OF FOR-
mer days do when they were not sleeping, eating, or on duty?
A number of pastimes are associated with the days of sail, of
which the most interesting is scrimshaw, the art of decorating ivory, bone,
or horn objects. This was accomplished by scratching patterns on the
object, and then enhancing them by rubbing in a dark pigment, usually

lampblack or ink. The art was commonly practiced on whaling vessels, where a whale tooth like this one readily provided a suitable object for decoration. Walrus tusks and other ivory or bone items were also used. The resulting artefact might be given to a family member or friend, or sold to augment the seaman's income. The design on this whale's tooth is a portrait of the Liverpool vessel *Rover*.

This scrimshaw carving not only exemplifies the skill of its maker, but also commemorates a significant episode in Liverpool's history. From the time of the Revolutionary War, American privateers marauded off the coast of Nova Scotia, targeting British ships. Privateers were authorized by their governments to seize and capture enemy merchant and naval vessels, along with their crew and cargo. A letter of marque was all the certification necessary for a ship's master to undertake actions that under normal circumstances would be considered piracy. Liverpool merchants' ships were subject to a great deal of harassment; they sustained so many losses that they in turn obtained letters of marque and retaliated by seizing American vessels and goods at every opportunity. The Court of Admiralty administered the proceeds from the spoils on behalf of the government, and the prize money awarded by the court to privateers was a major source of income to many Liverpool shipowners.

In 1799 Ichabod Darrow started to build a brig in his shipyard on the Mersey estuary, at what is now Brooklyn, for a consortium consisting of Simeon Perkins, Snow Parker, and William Lawson. The brig would take part in the privateering business. She was launched the following April and given the name *Rover*. While a basic brig was a two-masted and square-rigged vessel, *Rover* was also equipped with fore-and-aft sails at the stern and a boom to the mainmast. These features are skilfully depicted on the whale's tooth on display at the Queens County Museum. And the date inscribed on it, 1800, marks a significant event in the vessel's short history.

Under her captain, Alexander Godfrey, with a British letter of marque, *Rover* was one of the most successful Liverpool privateer vessels during her brief career. Her exploits became legendary within a short time of her launching. The most famous of these was her battle with the Spanish *Santa Rita* and three gunships off the coast of Venezuela in September 1800. *Santa Rita* was a well-armed naval schooner with a crew of 125— more than double that of the *Rover*. Nevertheless, the gunships were intimidated and retreated, and *Santa Rita* was boarded, captured, and brought back in triumph. Not one of the Liverpool men was lost, but 54 Spanish sailors were killed and *Rover* returned to port with 71 prisoners. Godfrey became an instant hero and was offered a commission in the Royal Navy. But he preferred a more independent life as captain of a trading vessel and refused the offer.

Rover's later career under a different captain was disappointing: she lost her letters of marque, and was sold in 1803 to Halifax merchants who used her as a trading vessel until she sank off the West Indies. Her privateering days were short, but memorable, and she is immortalized in this scrimshaw portrait.

Rover also lives on in other ways. Long after her days at sea, her exploits continued to fascinate people and became both part of the local folklore and a subject for writers. In "The Ballad of the Rover" published in 1919, Nova Scotia author and poet Archibald MacMechan celebrates her engagement with the *Santa Rita* in verse. Part of his dramatic account of the battle reads:

> *With muskets and with pistols we engaged them as they came*
> *Till they closed in port and starboard to play the boarding game;*
> *Then we manned the sweeps, and spun her round without a*
> *   thought of fear,*
> *And raked the Santa Rita from the Rover privateer.*
> *At once we spun her back again, the gunboats were too close;*
> *But our gunners they were ready, and they gave the dons*
> *   their dose.*
> *They kept their distance after that and soon away did sheer,*
> *And left the Santa Rita to the Rover privateer.*
> *We fought her for three glasses and then we went aboard,*

Our gallant captain leading us with pistol and with sword
It did not take us very long her bloody deck to clear,
And down came the Spanish colours to the Rover privateer.

A few years later, long-time Liverpool resident Thomas H. Raddall paid further tribute to the ship's memory with *The Saga of the Rover* (1931) and *The Rover: The Story of a Canadian Privateer* (1958).

Privateering remained a favourite and lucrative occupation of Liverpool shipowners for many years. The War of 1812 provided further opportunities, but international treaties developed later in the nineteenth century put a stop to the practice. Although its days are now long past, privateering lives on in the stories and memories of the people of Liverpool, and *Rover*'s short but brilliant career remains a highlight of the town's history. Each summer, the community hosts its annual Privateer Days Festival, with a variety of activities celebrating the heritage of the community. The festival attracts many visitors, so one might even say that privateering still contributes to Liverpool's prosperity.

~ 20 ~

Mi'kmaw woman's cap

19TH CENTURY

Glooscap Heritage Centre, Millbrook Reserve

NOVA SCOTIA'S NATIVE PEOPLE WORE GARMENTS MADE OF
furs and skins before white men came to Atlantic Canada. But
after contact with Europeans by the early seventeenth century,
the Mi'kmaq began to exchange their furs for wool and linen cloth, which

they used to make clothing. Their styles evolved as a result of the influence of fashions of the French and English settlers, but they continued to use traditional motifs to adorn these clothes.

Originally, Mi'kmaw skin-clothes were decorated with designs using paints and dyes made from ochres, charcoal, or ground shells, and embellished with natural items such as shells, animal teeth, and porcupine quills. Garments worn on ceremonial occasions like feasts and weddings were particularly elaborate. Once trading was established however, cloth replaced leather for clothing and new decorative items became available. Chief among these were little glass beads, which the Mi'kmaq used, along with ribbons and embroidery, in many different ways to replicate traditional patterns.

This peaked cap is a beautiful surviving example of the style of headdress made and worn by Mi'kmaw women during the eighteenth and nineteenth centuries, and perhaps even earlier. It is made of the dark blue woollen cloth most commonly used for Mi'kmaw women's clothing. The top comes to a point, and the lower part extends to the wearer's shoulders in the form of a hood, with a red band and elaborate trimming. Although the basic shape is very simple, the decorative design is elaborate and incorporates traditional Mi'kmaw motifs.

The basic design for the decoration of this cap is known as a double-curve pattern. Possibly based on the shape of the fiddlehead fern, it is a very common element in Mi'kmaw design. It has been found on articles of Mi'kmaw clothing and among the petroglyphs in Kejimkujik National Park. The pattern is used in various ways, on both the cap itself and its red border. The main pattern is worked in double rows of light-coloured beads against the dark background while the double curves are embellished with other decorative elements in beads of varying colours, mostly stylized representations of flowers and plants. There are also diagonal lines made of pairs of white and blue beads running through the main part of the cap, and curving lines on the red border. The coloured ribbons trimming the seams and the edges of the cap are also embroidered with beads. This cap would have taken many hours to create, and was probably intended for "best" wear on special occasions. For everyday wear, a woman's cap might be much simpler, perhaps with a plain beaded or ribbon border.

This woman's cap, exhibited in the Glooscap Heritage Museum, is an original nineteenth-century example of the fine design and craftsmanship practised by the Mi'kmaq. Although few of these garments have survived, caps of a similar style are still made and worn for ceremonial events.

~ 21 ~

German butter churn

C. 1800

Parkdale–Maplewood Community Museum, Maplewood

THE COMMUNITIES OF PARKDALE AND MAPLEWOOD LIE IN A
farming area of Lunenburg County northeast of New Germany.
Among the many interesting objects preserved in the area's
museum is this item, which looks at first glance more like a rocking
horse than a domestic appliance. Although made of wood, it bears little
resemblance to other wooden butter churns commonly found in early
country kitchens and dairies; these were mostly cylindrical, with a plunger,

or "dasher," which was raised and lowered by hand to agitate the cream and separate the butter fat from the liquid.

With a churn like this one, the early nineteenth-century housewife could make butter while she occupied herself with other things. Its design might be compared to that of a cradle, which could be rocked by a mother's foot, agitating the cream, while her hands were busy with her knitting or sewing, or tending a baby. It was a practical German design, brought to Lunenburg County by settlers in the 1750s. German immigrants originally lived in Lunenburg town for security, but many soon moved to their farm lots along the coast, and on nearby rivers and brooks.

In the first half of the nineteenth century, descendants of these settlers began to move beyond their original grants into the district known as New Germany, which then extended far beyond the present town of that name. It was an area of fertile farmland, and the pioneers made a good living farming and lumbering. Over towards Sherbroooke Lake, brothers Ezekiel and Henry Foster gave their name to what was for many years known as Foster Settlement, where they moved some time before 1848. The area where Ezekiel lived became known as Lower Foster Settlement, now Maplewood, while Henry's home, near Whetstone Lake, became Parkdale. Other families joined them, and later in the nineteenth century Judge DesBrisay described the area in his *History of the County of Lunenburg* as "one of the most improved agricultural districts in the area." He went on to write:

> The soil is good and many of the farms are first-class, while the dwellings and outbuildings show how well the farmers have succeeded. The farms of the Fosters, Wentzells, Fronks, and others are highly cultivated and yield good returns. One cannot drive through the settlement without being struck with its fine appearance and the wonderful advance which has been made since the brothers Foster first went there.

It was the Fronk family who brought with them this unusual butter churn. They were descendants of George Franck, a baker and miller who embarked for Nova Scotia with his wife in 1749 on the ship *Charlton,* among the earliest German immigrants brought here by Cornwallis. The first generation of Francks settled in Lunenburg, where they had a house and garden, and received a farm lot on the LaHave. Some of their descendants remained in that area, but others moved into the rapidly developing agricultural area of New Germany.

By the early nineteenth century the family name was written as "Fronk," but was later changed back to "Frank," as it is known in the area today. The area, too, changed its name, and, since Parkdale and Maplewood have developed as separate communities, is no longer known as Foster Settlement. But these two communities retain their historical ties, and their residents came together in the 1930s after "Uncle Tom" Spidell exhibited a collection of interesting items from his travels, in a local barn. The communities jointly built a museum, and when "Uncle Tom" died in 1963, he left his collection to the people of Parkdale–Maplewood. The museum and its collection were moved to its present location in the former Macabees Lodge Hall, which has since been considerably enlarged. Many of its artefacts reflect the early domestic and agricultural life of a rural society whose history goes back well over 150 years. The butter churn was passed down in the Fronk/Frank family until it was donated to the museum by Joseph Frank, and is a valuable reminder of a former way of life.

22

Davenport dessert plate

C. 1800–1816

Prescott House Museum, Starrs Point

S TANDING IN FINELY KEPT GARDENS ON STARRS POINT, BE-
tween the Cornwallis and Canard Rivers, is Prescott House. One
of Nova Scotia's stately homes, it was built by Charles Prescott,
whose father came to Halifax in the early 1750s. Charles was born in
1772 in Halifax, where he grew up, and by the turn of the century he had
become a prosperous merchant. In partnership with William Lawson,

Prescott's enterprises included overseas trading, and privateering during the Napoleonic Wars. He was active in the Halifax Committee on Trade, and supported the abortive project to establish a provincial joint stock bank in 1811. That same year, the partnership of Prescott, Lawson and Co. was dissolved, and the following year Charles left Halifax for health reasons, choosing the more salubrious air of Cornwallis Township.

On arriving in Cornwallis Township in 1812, Prescott purchased land overlooking the Cornwallis River and proceeded to build this fine Georgian house, which he called "Acacia Grove." Unlike most homes in rural Nova Scotia, it is made with local brick. It features a basement kitchen, four rooms on the ground floor and four upstairs, and servants' accommodation in the attic. Three years before the house was completed, Preston's first wife Hannah Whidden, with whom he had seven children, passed away. Prescott moved into this house in about 1816 with his second wife, Mariah Hammill, with whom he would have five more children. Among the possessions Mariah brought with her was a fine set of china.

The Prescotts enjoyed entertaining at Acacia Grove. Their guests included some of the leaders of Nova Scotia society, among them Lieutenant-Governor Lord Dalhousie, who wrote in July 1818, "At Mr. Prescott's, who is a very superior man indeed in manner, conversation and style of living to all others here, we met a large party at dinner." Perhaps their dessert was served on Mariah's floral dishes such as this one, which is now displayed in a Prescott House cabinet as part of her dessert service. Hand-painted on Davenport china made in Staffordshire, England, each plate is decorated with a different flower design—such as iris, lily, mallow, freesia and many others—executed in fine botanical detail. This example shows a convolvulus, commonly known as bindweed, related to the more exotic morning glory.

The botanical detail in these plates is particularly appropriate for Charles Prescott's household in the second phase of his career. As a country gentleman in Cornwallis, he took an active part in local affairs as a magistrate, churchwarden, school trustee, bridge commissioner, and, for a short time, MLA. In addition, he served on the legislative council for many years. He was also president of the local agricultural society and promoted scientific experimenting with farming methods, but one of his chief interests was landscape gardening.

Prescott was an enthusiastic horticulturalist and grew ornamental plants and shrubs on his property, cultivating the type of garden popular in England at the time, with lawns and formal flower beds. He had a special enthusiasm for fruit growing, laying out extensive orchards and building hot-houses where he grew a wide variety of fruit. As Susan Buggey writes in the *Dictionary of Canadian Biography*: "He cultivated apples, apricots, cherries, grapes, melons, nectarines, peaches, pears, plums, and strawberries. He reportedly grafted and tested more than 100 varieties of apples and nearly 50 varieties each of pears and plums, from which he willingly gave scions to other cultivators."

Prescott recognized the suitability of the region for the apple growing that would later become central to its identity. He brought in scions of many varieties, grafted them, and experimented to determine which ones would do well in the climate, introducing the Gravenstein and several other popular varieties. Joseph Howe, visiting the area in 1828, wrote enthusiastically about "Mr. Prescott's beautiful and extensive gardens, where every variety of fruit which the country will produce is blended with every flower, and where the perfection of modern horticulture may be viewed in successful operations."

As president of the Kings County Horticultural Society, Prescott was generous in sharing his knowledge and enthusiasm with others. He was one of the founders of the Nova Scotia Fruit Growers' Association (1863), and his work marks the beginning of the spread of fruit grow-ing in the Minas area and the Annapolis Valley. Today, two books from Charles Prescott's library can be seen at Prescott House: Robert Manning's *Book of Fruits* (Salem, 1838) and John Hull's *British Flora* (2nd ed., London, 1808). These books exemplify the consuming passions of a merchant-turned-horticulturalist who did so much to promote the fruit-growing industry that still forms an important part of the economy of the region.

When Charles Prescott died in 1859, the house was auctioned. The estate was well maintained for about thirty years by the subsequent owners, but then the property changed hands several times and the house eventually fell into a state of disrepair. Its contents were dispersed, and at one point it was used as lodgings for itinerant farm workers. Charles's great-granddaughter, Mary Allison Prescott, rescued Prescott House in 1931. During a visit to the area the previous year, Miss Prescott decided to buy the property and restore it to its former glory. Once she was able to negotiate its purchase, she began the task of restoring the house and furnishing it, in keeping with the period of its 1816 construction. She also began to look for some of the home's original contents. Among the items she was able to retrieve is the china dessert service now on display.

Miss Prescott created a small but beautiful garden and planted vines that clung to the walls of the house, where she lived with her two sisters from 1942 until her death in 1969. According to her wishes, the house became provincial property. Now managed by the Nova Scotia Museum, Prescott House retains the atmosphere of a family home, as it was almost two hundred years ago, when Mariah's dishes were brought out for dinner guests.

～23～

Gentleman's top hat

EARLY 1800S

McCulloch House Museum, Pictou

THIS TOP HAT ON DISPLAY IN PICTOU'S MCCULLOCH HOUSE
Museum was standard dress attire for nineteenth-century gentlemen. Made in Boston of black fur thought to be beaver, it once
adorned a very intelligent head.

Thomas McCulloch was born near Paisley, Scotland, in 1776. After
studying medicine at Glasgow University, he decided to prepare for the
ministry. He was ordained in the Secessionist branch of the Presbyterian

Church in 1799, and came to North America four years later. McCulloch had no intention of settling in Pictou when he left Scotland with his family. He had been commissioned to serve on Prince Edward Island, where he was bound when his ship put into Pictou Harbour late in 1803. Because of bad weather in the strait, he was forced to spend the winter in Pictou.

McCulloch found that the citizens of the newly established town were in need of a minister. They were Presbyterian Scots, many of whom had come to Nova Scotia on the *Betsy* in 1767 or the *Hector* in 1773. Among the town's leading citizens were merchants John Patterson, who in 1787 acquired the land on which the town was built, and Edward Mortimer, who arrived in Pictou the following year. After being joined by other merchants and shipbuilders, they began to develop the local economy based on the lumber industry. But when McCulloch arrived in 1803, there was still no minister in the growing town, and he was asked to stay.

The only clergy in the area prior to McCulloch were the Rev. Dr. James MacGregor and his colleague, the Rev. Duncan Ross. MacGregor had arrived from Scotland in 1786, and the following year he built two churches, one on the East River and one at Loch Broom on the West River, where a replica "Log Church" stands today. By the turn of the century, MacGregor ministered to the congregation on the East River, while Ross served the flock on the West River. Both ministers travelled widely to visit the scattered settlers, and from time to time preached in Pictou, but clearly another minister was needed to serve the increasing population of the town.

Thomas McCulloch accepted the challenge. He changed his plans and remained in Pictou, where the following year he was inducted as minister in what was then known as the Harbour Church, later the Prince Street Church. He served its congregation for twenty years, and, like his colleagues, travelled to outlying communities in need of a Presbyterian minister. He also preached and lectured in Halifax, where he was well liked—so much so that he was even invited to serve as minister, but his work in Pictou was deemed by the Associate Presbytery of Pictou to be more important.

McCulloch was acutely aware of the shortage of ministers in Nova Scotia and of the difficulty in recruiting enough Scottish clergy to serve its growing population. To him, the solution lay in providing a good liberal education within the colony and training homegrown ministers. While the sons of Anglicans could attend King's College in Windsor, non-conformists were not admitted. So, encouraged by MacGregor, McCulloch embarked on a project to educate promising young men beyond the basic "three Rs" (reading, writing, and arithmetic) and eventually prepare them for the ministry. Beginning with a group of boys whom McCulloch taught in his own home, this work was to occupy much of the rest of his life. With locally raised money, he first built a log schoolhouse on his own property. Unfortunately, it was destroyed by fire in 1814. But with MacGregor's support and some government funding, McCulloch created the institution that became the well-known Pictou Academy.

The Academy opened in 1818 with McCulloch as principal and MacGregor as a teacher. At the opening ceremony, McCulloch declared that education was one of the "best barriers against barbarism, and best rational system for the improvement in the world." The academy offered a liberal education, including both classics and science, and one wider in scope than that offered by King's. And it accepted students of all denominations, although the instructors were Presbyterian. It also offered courses in divinity, the first step towards training Nova Scotian students for the Presbyterian ministry. However, there was no degree-granting institution in Nova Scotia for non-Anglicans, meaning they had to leave the province in order to pursue formal university studies. So although the quality of education at Pictou Academy was high, its graduates had to go elsewhere to obtain a degree.

Sadly, the divisions within the Presbyterian Church laid obstacles in the way of McCulloch's ambitions. Disagreement among the Scottish clergy, and opposition from the Anglican establishment combined with the foundation of Dalhousie College (now University) as a non-denominational institution of higher learning, prevented the academy from obtaining degree-granting status. Disputes over the academy's status and financing continued for many years, until, in 1832, legislation provided funding for it to teach the "lower branches," while the "higher branches" would be taught at Dalhousie.

Disheartened, McCulloch continued to teach divinity for the Synod, but also began to search for some other way to use his skills as an educator. In 1838 he was appointed to Dalhousie as president, and professor of logic, rhetoric, and moral philosophy. After years of turmoil over religious and educational matters, this was a relatively calm period of McCulloch's life. He was always interested in natural history and had established a fine collection of wildlife specimens, some of which can be seen at Dalhousie's McCulloch Museum. The scholarly books that he brought with him to Halifax passed to the university on his death and today form part of the Special Collections of its Killam Memorial Library.

Though Thomas McCulloch chiefly worked as a minister and educator, he was also a naturalist, a collector, a lecturer, and writer of theological, scientific, and philosophical works. But his writing also had a lighter side. Today he is best known for the *Mephibosheth Stepsure Letters*, a collection of humorous observations on his fellow Nova Scotians, originally published in Halifax's *Acadian Reader* in the 1820s. The distinguished critic, Northrop Frye, hailed McCulloch as "the founder of genuine Canadian humour." He was indeed a man of many hats.

⁓ 24 ⁓

Scottish Presbyterian
Communion token

1808

Antigonish Heritage Museum

I F YOU PICKED UP THIS OBJECT IN THE STREET YOU MIGHT HAVE
a problem figuring out what it is. The small, oval metal disc—not
much bigger than a nickel—is not a coin, nor an identity disc (which it
somewhat resembles). It is a Communion token, an object intimately connected with the celebration of the Eucharist in the Scottish Presbyterian
Church, the Kirk of Scotland, to which a good number of early settlers
in the Antigonish area adhered.

Highland Scots came to the Antigonish area in the 1770s, and the
present town was established in 1784 by a group of Irish loyalists under
Capt. Timothy Hierlihy. Farther along the shore there were also Acadian
and Black Loyalist settlements. Thus from early days there was an ethnic
mix in the area, and also a religious mix. Although Antigonish is thought
of today as a primarily Roman Catholic community, the first church to
be built in what was then known as Dorchester was in fact Presbyterian,

founded to serve the local Scottish community two years before the Catholic chapel.

While Hierlihy's Irish followers were Roman Catholics, many of the Scottish settlers had Presbyterian roots and wished to continue with this familiar form of worship. In 1797 the Rev. James Munro visited Dorchester and conducted a service for the settlers' benefit, probably in the open air. In 1805 three Presbyterian settlers together donated an acre of ground in the town for a church, schoolhouse, and burying ground. The church was completed by 1808, and the Rev. James Munro was inducted as its first minister. Ten years later, the Rev. Thomas Trotter, who had begun his ministry in Johnshaven, Aberdeenshire, in Eastern Scotland, also in 1808, succeeded him.

Thomas Trotter spent the first ten years of his ministry in Johnshaven, where he was well respected, and served as clerk of the Aberdeen presbytery. But then, looking for a change, he accepted the call to Antigonish. He arrived with his family in June 1818. Like many of his neighbours he ran a farm and also built a gristmill and a fulling mill. A highly intelligent man interested in promoting education, he opened a grammar school the year after his arrival, for which he received an annual government grant of £100. There he taught Latin, Greek, and scientific subjects, and lectured and wrote on meteorology and geology as well as theological matters.

The minister brought with him this little oval disc, now preserved in the Antigonish Heritage Museum. On one side it reads, *ASSO. CON. JOHNS HAVEN* and on the other, *REVD. THOS. TROTTER 18.08*: his name, the date of his ordination, and the abbreviated name of the Associate Congregation of Johnshaven. As we see from its inscriptions, this token was made for use in the Rev. Thomas Trotter's Johnshaven parish.

The use of such tokens to identify the worthy members of the congregation goes back to the very beginning of Calvinism. In 1560 John Calvin suggested that "each person should receive tokens of lead for those of his household who were instructed; and the strangers who might come, on giving testimony of their faith, should also receive tokens, and those who had none should not be admitted to the tables." John Knox and his colleagues instituted this system of closed communion in Scotland, and it came to the New World with the migration of Scottish Presbyterians.

In eighteenth-century Scotland, and among the Scottish diaspora into the nineteenth-century Nova Scotia, Communion in Presbyterian congregations was not a weekly affair, but the culmination of a less frequent event often extending over several days. Participants came from a wide area, and in early days of settlement the gatherings were held in the open air and frequently conducted in Gaelic. A day of fasting, followed by a day of witness, theological discussion, and instruction, comprised the traditional preparation for Sunday's Communion. The Monday following was a day of thanksgiving before the assembly broke up. Receiving the sacrament was restricted to those whose conduct and beliefs proved them worthy, as identified by the minister or elders during the time of preparation. Each approved member was given one of these tokens. Whether in church or out of doors, participants had to present their token to one of the serving elders as proof of their eligibility to receive the bread and wine—only then were they allowed to sit at the common table where the elements were distributed.

The oval shape of this particular Communion token is typical of many such items, which could also be round, square, or oblong. They were made of varying types of metal—including, as Calvin suggested, lead, and the nature of their inscriptions also varies. Some, like this one, give the minister's name or initials and the name of the parish. Others have scriptural quotations or references, the image of a chalice or other symbols.

Thomas Trotter continued to serve his flock in Antigonish until his retirement in 1854, a year before his death. The token bearing his name and that of the parish where he began his ministry is a powerful reminder of the continuity between the religious practices of the Scottish Presbyterians in Nova Scotia and those of their land of origin.

~ 25 ~

Simeon Perkins's diary

1776–1811

Queens County Museum, Liverpool

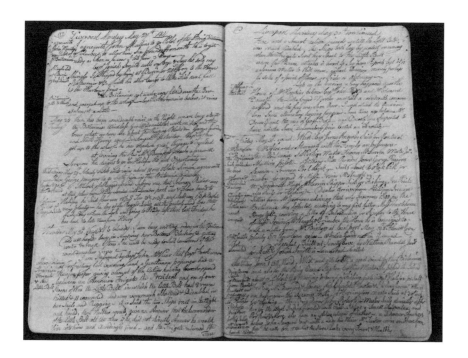

THESE PAGES ARE PART OF ONE OF TWENTY-SEVEN SURVIVING volumes of the diary kept by Simeon Perkins. Perkins was among the early Planter immigrants to Nova Scotia who came from New England in 1762 to the harbour known to the French as Port Rossignol. It was so named by Champlain after an enterprising French fishing captain who was caught there conducting trade with the Mi'kmaq, in defiance of the French king's grant of a trading monopoly to a favoured company. Rossignol's name remained with the river and the harbour for over 150 years, and his entrepreneurial spirit survived in the population of the town that the Planters renamed Liverpool.

Simeon Perkins was also an entrepreneur, and in the late eighteenth and early nineteenth centuries, promoted business development in the new community. He had interests in several local sawmills, and established a tannery. He was a merchant and ship owner, exporting lumber and fish to other parts of Canada and other, foreign ports. As well as attending to his business interests, he took a lively part in the affairs of the town and held various offices, including those of justice of the peace, judge, and member of the House of Assembly. He also outfitted privateering vessels during the American Revolutionary War and Napoleonic Wars.

Perkins maintained a record of his daily life and concerns and those of his fellow citizens from 1766, the period of early settlement, through the excitement of the privateering days, to the successful establishment of commerce and industry in the early nineteenth century. The diary's early pages detail the settlers' struggles to establish themselves and to set up businesses whereby they could become self-supporting and, eventually, prosperous. Settlers were dependent on supplies from elsewhere for much of their food, while their trading vessels, carrying exports of fish and lumber, returned with goods from the outside world. On Christmas Day 1773, when supplies failed to arrive, Perkins wrote, "I work in the woods. No fresh provisions, so I dine on salt fish." And because in Perkins's time the weather affected people's lives even more than it does today, he kept a daily record of that as well. Natural disasters were not uncommon. On Friday, December 19, 1766, when ice filled the channel after several days of snow, he wrote, "Heavy rains, and wind E. and E. S. E. The upper saw mill dam was washed out in the middle during the night."

The two pages featured in this book are from a later volume of the diary, and were written between Monday, May 27, and Saturday, June 1, 1811, towards the end of Perkins's life, when his affairs had prospered and the town of Liverpool was well established. They detail key elements of the week's events, and read rather like a local weekly newspaper: included are a weather report, shipping news, news from out of town, and local and social news. They also record some of Perkins's personal affairs.

Monday's entry records Perkins's hiring John Mullins as a pilot for his ship *Britannia*'s forthcoming voyage to Quebec. It would be a quick turnaround, as *Britannia* had "fetched over the bar and warped up to the wharf" that day from Trinidad, and Perkins wanted her away again in three days. The next few days were spent on maintenance. On Thursday, Perkins was "busy writing Orders for the Britannia, and all hands busy in Scraping her Bottom, Blacking and getting water & Small Stores. She will be ready to sail tomorrow if the wind and weather serves."

The comings and goings of several other ships carrying both merchandise and passengers are recorded during the week, their various destinations including Halifax, Montreal, Quebec, and the West Indies. We learn the names of the ships' masters, and sometimes those of the crew. The departure of several fishing vessels is also noted. Incoming vessels bring news of the outside world: "I am informed by Capt. John McVicar," Perkins writes on Thursday, "that Capt. Frost was at Port Metway last Evening and a Gentleman passenger had a Halifax paper giving account of an Action having happened between an American Frigate the President and one of our Sloops of War the Little Belt...." He goes on to recount the details of the incident, a precursor of the War of 1812. Meanwhile, back in Liverpool that evening, "a fray happened near the House of Mr Hopkins between Capt. John Barss and Mr. Edward Dewolf. The latter cryed [sic] Murder on which a considerable concourse gathered and the fray was soon over. I understand the Occasion was some Altercation having happened some time ago between Mr. DeWolf and the wife of Capt. Barss." The Barss family were respectable Liverpool citizens, and it seems that DeWolf had written something defamatory about one of them.

On Friday, two vessels leave Liverpool: Captain James Knowles sails for Montreal, and Perkins's *Britannia* heads for Quebec. By an incoming vessel the same day, Perkins writes, "I receive Letters from Mr. Yeoman advising that my insurance £1300 on the Britannia was Expected according to my first letter...." A careful businessman, he records the state of the market for flour and corn, which are plentiful, adding, "W. India goods not in demand." The launching of "a vessel built at Sandy Cove by Nathaniel Randall Junr. For Nath. & Josiah Smith" is also noted. We learn that a fishing vessel sailing on Saturday was to put in to Halifax for salt, its passengers including the former minister, whose farewell sermon Perkins mentions earlier. And the week closes satisfactorily, with the arrival of a schooner bringing "John Sargent Esq. with a Lady his Niece. Mr Tucker comes on Shore from her he calls on me at the Store Looks very Smart and Healthy." Similar kinds of details would be found in a small town newspaper for many years afterwards.

The varied events and personalities recorded in these pages of Perkins's diary reflect a week in the life of a busy community in which trading, fishing, and shipbuilding played an important role. They open a window on Liverpool's commercial and social life, and on the wide range of Perkins's interests. This is a valuable document in the history of the town and a true treasure for Queens County Museum.

~ 26 ~

Thomas Davison's letter book

1812

Wallace and Area Museum, Wallace

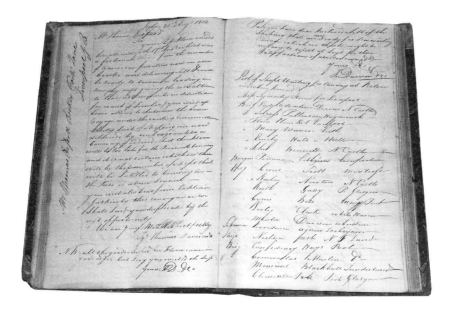

HOW DID A PICTOU BUSINESSMAN'S LETTER BOOK COME TO be on display at the Wallace and Area Museum, some seventy-five kilometres to the west?

Thomas Davison, a merchant, lumber dealer, and shipbuilder, lived in Pictou, where he had set up business in 1803. He bought lumber of all kinds from many small communities along the Northumberland Strait—including the village of Wallace—for sale internationally, and kept copies of his business correspondence in this book. The two pages shown here contain records from the time of the War of 1812, when ships were being blockaded in Nova Scotia harbours by American privateers.

Davison's letter to a Liverpool broker details the cargo vessel he is loading and preparing for departure, and its insurance. He writes of the problems with the privateers, and of the convoys assembled in Pictou harbour to ensure the safe passage of trading vessels. These pages also contain the names of vessels in the harbour awaiting the formation of such a convoy, and their destinations. The list demonstrates the variety of British ports to which Nova Scotia's merchant fleet sailed: they were bound for Liverpool, Newcastle, Leith, Hull, Weymouth, Montrose, Glasgow, Maryport, Whitehaven, Aberdeen, Loch Ryan, Poole, and Sunderland, along with one for Newfoundland.

Thomas's sons, James and David Davidson, were probably travelling with their father on business when they first saw the village of Wallace. Mi'kmaq had known the area for thousands of years and given it the name *Remsheg*, meaning "the place between." Some Acadian families came to settle there in 1710, and the dykes they built to protect their farmland can still be seen. Their proximity to Île Saint-Jean (PEI) made the harbours on the north shore good locations from which supplies could be shipped by the Acadians to their compatriots on the island, and as far afield as Louisbourg. This trade made the Acadians of Remsheg particularly unpopular with the government in Halifax, and on August 15, 1755, they were among the first to be uprooted from their homes, their houses burnt and their farms abandoned, as the Deportation began.

The settlement was re-established in the 1780s, when a group of Loyalist families obtained land in what was known as the Remsheg Grant, which extended from Wallace River to Malagash Point. They worked the old Acadian farms, fished in the Northumberland Strait, and cut and sawed lumber for construction, shipbuilding, and trade. Shipbuilding remained an important business along the Northumberland Shore for much of the nineteenth century, and during its heyday in the mid-1850s there were a dozen shipyards in Wallace. From small fishing boats to large trading schooners, the community's vessels supported other elements of the local economy. Wallace Harbour was important for the export not only of fish and lumber, but also of the fine stone quarried a short distance upriver.

A father of eleven, Thomas was an apparently respectable citizen of Pictou, until in 1817 he caused a scandal by abandoning his family and heading off to Boston with the widow of another Pictou businessman. To support the family, James and David, Thomas's elder sons, maintained his shipbuilding business, while their mother, with the help of her children, opened a boarding house and became a successful businesswoman in her own right. With the help of his brother James, David began to build ships in Pictou the year after his father's departure. The two also gained experience as sailors and became master mariners.

In 1837 the two brothers left Pictou to set up new enterprises. James came to Wallace, where in 1839 he purchased a fine lot overlooking the shore, originally granted to Peter Tuttle, and built himself a comfortable family home. He was married in 1841 to Lavinia Dickson, with whom he would have five children. With backing from a local merchant—a relative of his new wife—James established the Davison Shipyard on the shore below his house. David soon joined him. The brothers were among Wallace's leading businessmen, building ships, trading in lumber, and operating a general store. James was responsible for the business operations in Wallace, while David, who remained unmarried, oversaw the building of the vessels, which he then sailed to England, laden with lumber, returning with manufactured goods for sale in the store.

James's position in the community developed as he took a leading role in the local religious, political, and social life. He was appointed Controller of Customs in 1850 and in 1855 became the local Surveyor of Shipping. He also kept close ties with family members in Pictou. The prosperity of the region fluctuated according to the demand for its products, and shipbuilding suffered in the second half of the nineteenth century with the decline of the age of sail. In Wallace, diminishing activity at the Davison's shipyard coincided with David's death in 1860. James maintained the business, but quickly sold off his vessels and finally closed the shipyard in 1868. The store continued for a few years more, and James died in 1894.

The next generation of Davisons was not interested in continuing the family businesses. Two of James's sons moved away, while a third son, Robert, remained in Wallace and became a farmer. The house was kept within the family and eventually came into the possession of James's great-grandson, John Alexander Kennedy, who bequeathed it to the community for use as a museum. This letter book was preserved by Thomas Davison's descendants and is one of the Wallace and Area Museum's many treasures. It remains today the opening chapter in the history of one of the community's leading families.

～ 27 ～

Portrait of Lieutenant Provo William Parry Wallis, by Robert Field

1813

Art Gallery of Nova Scotia, Halifax

T HIS OIL PAINTING, HELD IN THE ART GALLERY OF NOVA Scotia, brings together two men who pursued very different careers in early nineteenth-century Nova Scotia. Their paths crossed in 1813 in Halifax, where artist Robert Field painted a portrait of a handsome young naval officer, Provo Wallis. At this time, Halifax was both the capital of a rapidly developing Nova Scotia and an important base for the Royal Navy.

British-born Field had studied art in London, attending the Royal Academy schools in 1790. Four years later, he emigrated from Britain to the United States with a number of other artists, hoping to make a living. He lived first in Baltimore and then in Philadelphia, Washington, and Boston, and became successful as a miniaturist. His subjects included George and Martha Washington, Thomas Jefferson, and other eminent Americans. Field was living in Boston when relations between Britain and the United States deteriorated leading up to the War of 1812. In 1808 he moved to Nova Scotia, where he had success for some years both with his miniatures and larger portraits of prominent members of an increasingly sophisticated Halifax society. These included two lieutenant-governors, the bishop, the vice admiral, and other dignitaries.

Robert Field's name appears on a grant of land made in 1812 at Coldstream, along the old Cobequid Road, where his brother William also received a grant. Their lots adjoined that of a colourful character, Sir John Oldmixon, an English theatrical personality once known as "the Beau of Bath," who left England to escape heavy debts, moved to Philadelphia where he left his actress wife, then came to Nova Scotia and established a second family. Oldmixon and William Field built houses and settled on their country properties. A small artistic community might have developed at Coldstream, but Robert remained in Halifax where he was an active member of fashionable society, making contacts with the ladies and gentlemen who became the subjects of his paintings. But Halifax was still a small town with a limited number of people wealthy enough to commission portraits, and rural Nova Scotia offered few prospects. Faced with a diminishing market, Field abandoned Nova Scotia for Jamaica in 1816, hoping for more potential clients. His time there was short; he died, probably of yellow fever, in 1819.

Halifax-born Provo Wallis, the subject of this portrait, came from a family with a long-standing connection to the British Navy. His grandfather was a naval shipwright who settled in Halifax after serving in the Seven Years' War and the American Revolutionary War. His father also worked in the Naval Dockyard, and young Provo, born in 1791, was destined for the Navy from an early age. Like many of his generation, he was sent to school in England; but at the age of thirteen, he began his naval service. He advanced rapidly, being appointed acting lieutenant in 1806 and promoted to full lieutenant in 1808, the same year Robert Field came to Halifax. Two years later Lieutenant Provo Wallis saw action in the capture of Guadeloupe, for which he received a medal.

Simmering disputes between Britain and the Americans came to a head in 1812, when the Americans declared war on their former colonial masters. The onset of hostilities found Wallis serving as second lieutenant on board the British frigate HMS *Shannon,* under the command of Captain Broke, in the North Atlantic. In June 1813, Wallis participated in the most famous of *Shannon*'s exploits: the seizing of the American frigate *Chesapeake* outside Boston Harbor. The British ship had been blockading the harbour when *Chesapeake* came out to challenge her. In the ensuing battle, the gunnery practice in which Broke had drilled his crew paid off: *Chesapeake* was quickly crippled, but at the cost of many lives on both sides. A British crew took over the enemy vessel, but Captain Broke had sustained a serious head wound, and the first lieutenant was killed in action. Lieutenant Provo Wallis was left to take responsibility for his ship and her prize. He saw to the repairs of both vessels and brought them safely back to Halifax, where he received a hero's welcome. Captain Broke was brought ashore, where Wallis arranged for his care, and he eventually recovered from his injury.

That same year, Robert Field painted this portrait of the now famous Lieutenant Wallis. It is a sensitive painting of a good-looking, pleasant, young naval officer with a half-smile on his face, which supports Captain Broke's assessment of him as "an amiable young man."

After his return to Halifax, Wallis quickly received a promotion to commander and continued a successful naval career, first here and then in the Mediterranean, before returning to Britain to serve as aide-de-camp to Queen Victoria. In 1851 he was made rear admiral, and for a short time in 1857 was commander-in-chief of British ships off the coast of South America. Back in England after more than fifty years of active service, he received a knighthood in 1860 and continued to gain naval promotions, being named Vice Admiral of the United Kingdom from 1870–1876, and finally Admiral of the Fleet in 1877.

Provo Wallis died in England at the age of one hundred, as the last surviving commanding officer of the Napoleonic Wars. Much of his life had been spent at sea or in England, but he is remembered in Nova Scotia for his exploits while based in Halifax. In 1969 a new vessel built for the Canadian Coast Guard fleet was named *Provo Wallis* in his honour. She was a familiar sight on the Dartmouth waterfront until being transferred to British Columbia in 2006.

Today Canada has its own navy and Nova Scotia a thriving homegrown artistic community. Field's portrait of Provo Wallis is a fine example of his skill in portraiture. It reflects a period when Nova Scotians served in the British Navy and British-trained artists painted portraits of our local dignitaries, of which this portrait of a Nova Scotia-born hero is a particularly valuable example.

~28~

Great Highland
and "Waterloo" bagpipes

DATE UNKNOWN; 1815

Celtic Music Interpretive Centre, Judique

THESE TWO OLD SETS OF BAGPIPES SYMBOLIZE THE MUSICAL tradition brought by the Highland Scottish settlers to Cape Breton in the late eighteenth century. They can be found in the museum attached to the Celtic Music Interpretive Centre in Judique on

Cape Breton's west coast, which claims to be Cape Breton's oldest Scottish settlement. Through its displays, the centre celebrates Cape Breton's musical history and perpetuates and nurtures its traditions with classes and workshops in piping and fiddling.

In Scottish history, bagpipes can be traced back to the Middle Ages. They were sometimes referred to as "warpipes" because of the practice of carrying them into conflict to inspire the men who followed them and to intimidate their foes. Pipe music was used as a call to battle, as an incentive to fight bravely, and, in the aftermath, as a lament to mourn the fallen. After the Battle of Culloden (1746), when Jacobite supporters of Bonnie Prince Charlie were defeated and mercilessly killed by English soldiers, attempts were made by the British authorities to weaken the Scottish clan system. They outlawed many Highland traditions, including dress and language, but strangely the pipes were not forbidden. Indeed, Highlanders were recruited as part of the British fighting forces in the late eighteenth century, and soon afterwards pipers were enlisted to lead their regiments into battle.

Bagpipes were, at this time, considered by many to be weapons of war; their sound terrorized the enemy. The tradition of sending pipers into the battlefield continued for many years, though casualties were high among them, and the practice became less common because of this. Nevertheless, the pipes were heard again in the Second World War during the decisive Battle of El Alamein (1942). Today the bagpipes are an integral part of the regimental bands of Highland units, both in the United Kingdom and the Commonwealth. Although they have no place in modern warfare, bagpipes are still commonly used for ceremonial purposes. We hear their music in parades, and "The Flowers of the Forest" is still played at funerals and remembrance ceremonies.

In the 1780s Scottish landowners began turning their hillsides over to sheep and many impoverished crofters immigrated to Cape Breton, bringing their music and dancing with them. Highlanders were accustomed to making their own entertainment at ceilidhs and kitchen parties, and this practice continued in their new communities. Here, the pipes were used for peaceful purposes, a reminder of the homeland and an accompaniment to many social occasions. Composition is considered a desirable skill among pipers, and traditional tunes have been augmented over the years by music composed on this side of the Atlantic.

The set of Great Highland Bagpipes shown here on the left once belonged to Father Raymond Gerard MacDonald, who was born in Antigonish and served as priest in several Cape Breton parishes until his retirement in 2002. MacDonald also played the piano and the accordion, and must have been much in demand at parish festivities.

The second set of pipes, on the right, is older, and was brought from Scotland to Cape Breton in 1815 by Iain Gillis, a pioneer settler at Ben Eoin. They are known as the "Waterloo Pipes," because it was said that they were played at the Battle of Waterloo. They were passed down through Gillis's family to his son, Sim an Tailleac, and then to Sim's nephew, Rhuairidh MacIsaac, who played both pipes and fiddle. Hughie MacIntyre, who served as a piper in the North Nova Scotia Highlanders during the Second World War, later bought the pipes. They then passed to his cousin, Father Allan J. MacMillan of Judique, and finally to the museum.

Both sets of pipes consist of a chanter, three drones held in position by a cord, and a "bag," which, when in use, is filled with air by means of a blowpipe. The chanter is a reed instrument, played with both hands to produce a melody. The drones are also reeded, and provide continuous background notes against which the tune is played. The "bag" is tucked under the arm and pumped, providing a steady flow of air to the chanter and the drones during performance.

The musical traditions that came with the early settlers continue to flourish and develop in Cape Breton. Fiddle music, like pipe music, was a strong tradition in the Scottish Highlands and produced many notable musicians. Immigrants brought with them their instruments and their traditional tunes, many of which—like jigs and reels—were used for dancing, while slower airs might bring tears to the eyes of listeners. While the pipes are usually played out of doors, the fiddle is frequently the instrument of choice at the ceilidhs and kitchen parties that are part of the island's social life.

Today, Cape Breton fiddle music has been enriched by the influence of Irish and Acadian traditions, and has developed a style of its own. The island has been home to many well-known musicians and composers, whose lives are celebrated in Judique both on the museum walls and in recordings. They include old-timers like Little Jack MacDonald, Dan Rory MacDonald, his nephews John Allan and John Don Cameron, and Hugh Allan "Buddy" MacMaster, as well as more recent celebrities like Buddy's niece Natalie MacMaster, famous for her fiddling and step-dancing, J. P. Cormier, an Acadian singer-songwriter from Chéticamp, and Ashley MacIsaac, the well-known fiddler from Creignish.

The fiddles and bagpipes that early settlers brought with them laid the foundations of a strong musical tradition among their descendants. Today, Cape Breton's music is no longer limited to traditional instruments, but continues to attract visitors from across Canada and beyond to its annual Celtic Colours Festival and other musical events. These two sets of bagpipes in Judique's museum remind us how it all started.

～ 29 ～

Richard John Uniacke's
walking stick

C. 1815

Uniacke Estate Museum Park, Mount Uniacke

THIS LONG BAMBOO WALKING STICK, WITH its metal ferrule and curly ram's horn at the top, can be seen at Mount Uniacke, a dignified Georgian house on the old Windsor Road. The estate is located midway between Halifax and Windsor, on the old Post Road that was the first of Nova Scotia's main highways. It was here, in 1815, that its owner, Richard John Uniacke, assumed the life of a country gentleman.

The Uniackes were an old Irish Protestant family with a home in County Cork called Mount Uniacke. Richard John was born there in 1753, educated in Lismore, and as a young man articled to a Dublin lawyer. Here he espoused the cause of the Irish nationalists, much to the displeasure of his father, and as a result of this family dispute he left Ireland in 1773 for the West Indies. From there Richard John travelled to Philadelphia, where he met Moses Delesdernier, with whom he formed a business partnership and came to Nova Scotia in 1774. The following year he married Delesdernier's daughter, Martha, who was only twelve years old at the time. The marriage was not consummated immediately, but the couple eventually had six sons and six daughters before Martha's death in 1803. He married again in 1808, and his second wife, Eliza Newton, gave him one more son.

Always opinionated when it came to politics, Uniacke had a brief brush with the law in Nova Scotia in 1776, when he was arrested for supporting an uprising on the Chignecto Isthmus. Influential friends secured his release, and he returned to Ireland to complete his legal studies, qualifying as an attorney in Dublin in 1779. Back in Halifax, he was admitted to the bar in 1781, and embarked on a long legal and political career. He was appointed solicitor general that same year, and two years later was elected to the House of Assembly. Uniacke's great wish was to become attorney general, but his clashes of opinion with an influx of ambitious Loyalists meant that this wish would go unfulfilled for some time. Meanwhile, he was next appointed advocate general of the Court of Vice-Admiralty. In 1789 he became speaker of the Assembly, but at this time Nova Scotia was a hotbed of political rivalry, the scramble for patronage appointments was intense, and he did not run for re-election in 1793. In 1797 the position of attorney general once more became vacant, and this time Uniacke's ambition was realized. He successfully sought re-election to the Assembly, and once more became speaker. He retired from that office in 1805, but continued to play an active role in Nova Scotia politics as a member of the legislative council.

The War of 1812 saw a revival of the privateering that had taken place during the American Revolutionary War. Uniacke's position at the Court of Vice-Admiralty was very lucrative, as he drew fees from the processing of prize claims, and by the end of the war he was a wealthy man with a fortune of £50,000. For much of his working life, Uniacke had lived in a townhouse in Halifax, but now he could afford to fulfill another dream: to own a country estate. It is said that he had observed this site on the Windsor Road many years ago, while being brought to Halifax under arrest for supporting the 1776 Chignecto uprising, and was reminded of his Irish childhood home. Now he was in a position to acquire the land, and build a second Mount Uniacke. The estate was completed in 1815.

The house stands beside the lake Uniacke named after his first wife, Martha. Its garden was nicely landscaped and protected by a ha-ha, a kind of ditch designed to be invisible from the house, but deep enough to prevent straying beasts from the farm or forest from encroaching on the lawn and flower beds. The house was built for comfort and entertaining, and its well-proportioned rooms were richly furnished with pieces made by a London cabinetmaker. Uniacke loved company, and in the days of slow travel by horse-drawn carriages or sleighs, his location on the Windsor Road allowed him to offer hospitality to travelling friends or distinguished guests in the form of a meal in the gracious dining room, or a bed for the night in the ground-floor guest room. Lord Dalhousie was a frequent visitor during his governorship, and observed in his journal that Mount Uniacke was "the only Gentleman's seat on the road."

Uniacke's library is on the ground floor of the house. Here are walls lined with books, his enormous chair, his desk, and nearby, this walking stick that accompanied him as he strolled round his estate. The story goes that Uniacke had among his livestock a favourite bull, for whom he always carried a treat in his pocket. One day, no doubt with his mind on other matters, he forgot the treat, and the disappointed bull charged him and knocked him down. But the bull had picked the wrong opponent. Uniacke was a giant of a man, and not easily intimidated. Getting up with the help of this walking stick, he found the bull advancing on him again, so he whacked it hard on the nose with the ram's horn end, temporarily stunning the beast. Uniacke went on his way, and neither he nor the stick seems to have suffered from the encounter.

Following Richard John Uniacke's death in 1830, the estate remained home to the Uniacke family for seven generations, and is now part of the Nova Scotia Museum family. The original elegant furnishings as well as personal items, such as this stick, provide a glimpse of the lifestyle of an early nineteenth-century country gentleman, who enjoyed comfortable living and entertained lavishly.

～ 30 ～

Mrs. Mary Ross's teacup and saucer

1816

Ross Farm Museum, New Ross

A SIMPLE CUP AND SAUCER STAND IN THE CENTRE OF THE
parlour table at Rosebank Cottage at the Ross Farm Museum.
They are the last vestiges of the tea set brought to the settlement
of Sherbrooke (now New Ross) by Mrs. Mary Ross in 1816.

After the War of 1812, Mary's husband, Captain William Ross, accepted the captaincy of the disbanded men of the Nova Scotia Fencibles

who were prepared to remain in Nova Scotia. Ross was to supervise their settlement. In order to encourage development and expand the colony's population to inland areas, land was surveyed and lots were laid out along a newly cut section of the Halifax–Annapolis Road at Gold River. As Lord Dalhousie recounts in his journal,

> they were offered land and rations; about 100 families accepted & came into this wilderness. Mr. Ross, an Irishman, resolved on sharing their hardships and has done a great deal in the way of example & by encouragement, but from want of system on the part of Government when first placing them here, they have had to contend with the most appalling difficulties.
> (*The Dalhousie Journals*, August 1, 1818)

This was written on the occasion of Dalhousie's visit to the settlement two years after it had been initiated. He travelled on horseback from Chester Basin over a road that after five kilometres deteriorated to the point when "what with rocks & bogs & rotten trees I could never have hoped to accomplish the end without broken legs or arms."

It was over such a road that the Sherbrooke settlers struggled, along with their possessions. They had to clear land to build dwellings and to grow crops for subsistence once the initial supply of rations had ceased. Not all the men allotted grants stayed to develop them, but those who did formed the community we now call New Ross. The settlement was extremely isolated. Travellers from Halifax went by sea to Chester, then overland by the unsatisfactory route described above by Lord Dalhousie. It was many years before this road became passable for wheeled vehicles.

William Ross brought with him his wife, Mary, his daughter, Mary, and sons William, Edward, and George. As the leader of the community, William Ross was granted a large tract of land in a pleasant location overlooking a lake just south of the Annapolis Road. There he built a log cabin for immediate shelter, and then the frame house he named Rosebank, which is still standing. A fourth son, Lawson, was born there in February 1818. When the Ross family received Lord Dalhousie at Rosebank that summer, Mrs. Ross likely offered tea to His Lordship in this very cup, or a similar one, from her best tea set.

Lord Dalhousie maintained contact with the Ross family and, according to Judge DesBrisay's account in his *History of the County of Lunenburg*, "bestowed upon them many substantial tokens of regard." Among these gifts was a piano, which he gave to young Mary Ross before leaving Nova Scotia to take up his duties as governor general of Upper and Lower Canada. Stalwart soldiers carried the piano up the hazardous trail from the coast so that it might take its place in the parlour at Rosebank, where it still stands, together with an old family violin.

The settlers had been promised that the Annapolis Road would be completed to provide direct access to Halifax by way of Hammonds Plains. Hoping to advance this project, William Ross set out in the fall of 1821 with a Mi'kmaw guide in search of a potential route through the wilderness. Judge DesBrisay takes up the story:

> They got benighted in the woods, and were overtaken by a violent rainstorm. The captain lay all night exposed to the fury of the elements, with naught but a wet log for his pillow. He was taken very ill and had to remain a few days at Sherwood Lodge, his sickness culminating in violent disease, from the effects of which he died in Halifax, May 2nd, 1822, leaving his wife, with a young family, to buffet the world, thousands of miles away from her native land. (*History of the County of Lunenburg*)

Mrs. Ross was pregnant at the time of her husband's death, and another son, James, was born the following September. Their daughter, Mary, was only fourteen years old; their eldest son, William, twelve; Edward, nine; George, seven; and Lawson only four. Somehow, with the help of friends and neighbours, they all survived.

We know little of the Ross family's existence in the years immediately following Captain Ross's death. Mary married Andrew Kiens, the son of one of her father's fellow officers, and they lived on the far side of the lake. William married Rachel Floyd, who took part in household activities with her mother-in-law. In 1835, Edward, now in his early twenties, began to keep a diary. It tells of daily life on the farm, which George operated, with the seasonal seeding and harvesting, mowing hay, and tending livestock, in which family, friends, and neighbours all took part. George occupied rainy days making and repairing shoes. William ran a saw- and gristmill with help from his brothers. Edward operated a store, which he stocked on journeys to Halifax. And Lawson and James helped their brothers. Together the Ross men all worked on road maintenance, to make it possible to reach the coast—by wagon in summer, and by sled in winter. The women kept busy with household activities: cooking, carding and spinning, making and mending clothes.

Members of the Ross family worked hard, but they also enjoyed a full social life after work. Edward's journal tells of many gatherings in the cottage, from quiet family teas to full-blown parties with music, singing, and dancing, where liquor flowed and the young people flirted. (The people of Sherbrooke knew how to have a good time.) Somehow, Mrs. Ross's cup and saucer survived all the activity and are among the treasures of Rosebank Cottage, now part of the Ross Farm Museum, where the public can experience a taste of early nineteenth-century farm life.

～31～

Joseph Howe's printing press

1819

Nova Scotia Archives, Halifax

I N THE FOYER OF THE NOVA SCOTIA ARCHIVES BUILDING, THIS old iron printing press stands alongside a row of computers. In a few years' time the computers will have become obsolete, replaced by newer models, and discarded. But this press will continue to be preserved because of the important part it played in Nova Scotia's history.

From Gutenberg's time in the fifteenth century onwards, texts have been printed on presses that allow multiple copies to be produced at ever-increasing speeds. While they have varied in design over the years, until recently, commercial presses all operated on the same principle: type was set, letter by letter, and transferred to the press, where ink was applied. A sheet of paper was laid on top of the type and pressure was applied, transferring the ink to the paper. This process is known as letterpress printing. Mechanized presses were developed during the nineteenth century, but the principle on which they operated remained the same for many years. Originally, printing presses were wooden, like the wine presses from whose design they were adapted, but by the nineteenth century metal had replaced wood. This early nineteenth-century press is similar to the original Gutenberg design and operates the same way.

A printer named Bartholomew Green brought the first printing press to Halifax, from Boston, in 1751. While Green unfortunately died soon after his arrival, his business associate, John Bushell, took over his press and type and set up a printing shop on Grafton Street. It was here that the first newspaper in Canada, *The Halifax Gazette*, was printed in 1752. It was well received, and soon other newspapers sprang up to rival it in popularity. The *Gazette*, also the official source of government announcements, was followed in 1769 by *The Nova Scotia Chronicle and Weekly Advisor*, printed by Anthony Henry. And more would come. Numerous printers were working in the downtown area by the mid-nineteenth century, and not only newspaper publishers. The Halifax printing industry grew quickly: some printers were stationers, selling ruled ledgers and account books; some printed books; and some were booksellers. They also executed private orders.

One of Halifax's early printers was John Howe, also from Boston, a Loyalist who established a print shop on the corner of Barrington and Sackville Streets in 1780. There, he published a newspaper, *The Halifax Journal*. Howe was the most successful of the Halifax printers of his day, and in 1801 he was appointed King's Printer, responsible for printing official government documents. But it is his son Joseph, born in 1804, who is now remembered as one of Nova Scotia's distinguished printers, publishers, and journalists, and this is his press.

The press was designed and patented in 1819 by John Wells of Hartford, Connecticut, and Joseph, who had established his own printing business, bought it in the 1820s from a fellow Halifax printer. It served him well. Marjorie Whitelaw summarizes Howe's printing career in her book, *First Impressions*:

> On this machine in 1829 Joe Howe printed Thomas Chandler Haliburton's *An Historical and Statistical Account of Nova-Scotia,* and later, in 1835–36, the famous satirical sayings of Sam Slick of Slickville, one of Canada's earliest works of lasting literary significance. On this machine Joe Howe, as publisher of *The Novascotian*, printed the editorials in which he developed his political philosophy; this was the very press on which the mighty battle for responsible government was argued and won.

This brings us to the importance of the press in Howe's political career and in the history of Nova Scotia. As a young man, Howe was constantly widening his horizons. As a journalist, he became interested in politics as he attended and reported on sessions of the House of Assembly. He also explored the province, describing his journeys in columns printed in *The Novascotian* entitled "Western Rambles" and "Eastern Rambles." But it was Howe's political editorials, produced on this press, that brought him to prominence—particularly one printed in 1835, in which he denounced the Halifax police and magistrates for unjustly extorting money from the citizens. He was sued for libel, and famously defended himself in an oratorical feat lasting more than six hours, before a court that was held in what is now the Legislative Library of Province House. His defence speech won him an acquittal from the jury as well as a reputation for defending the freedom of the press.

Howe went on to a political career in which he stood up for the interests of citizens against the self-interest of officials. He was first elected as a member of the Assembly in 1836 and became speaker in 1841. He continued to write for *The Novascotian* and *Morning Chronicle*, and his editorials between 1854 and 1856 vigorously promoted the Reform Party's efforts to achieve responsible government for the province. The highlight of his career was a successful campaign that made Nova Scotia the first of the British colonies to achieve this status. Howe is also remembered for his promotion of the Nova Scotia Railway, the province's first, which linked Halifax with Windsor and Truro. A government-sponsored project, incorporated in 1853, the two branches were opened in 1858.

Howe fought many political battles, notably against Sir Charles Tupper, with whom he disagreed over Confederation, but eventually he accepted the inevitable and became a member of the newly formed Dominion government. Already in poor health, in 1873 Joseph Howe became lieutenant-governor of Nova Scotia. He died shortly after his appointment, after a long and varied career. Today, Howe's name is familiar to all Nova Scotians: in Halifax, a street, a school, an apartment house, a downtown business building, and a room in Province House all bear it. A commemorative statue stands in the Province House grounds, and his grave in Camp Hill Cemetery is signposted for visitors.

Fine letterpress printing is now carried on by a small number of dedicated enthusiasts operating private presses, while commercial printers have embraced the rapidly developing techniques that have emerged since the mid-twentieth century. Computers are used to produce newspapers, books, and other printed material, and even the traditional book is giving way to electronic devices. But Joe Howe's press remains a tangible reminder both of his personal achievements and of a method of disseminating information that has been in use for over five hundred years.

∼ 32 ∼

Antique French wallpaper

C. 1820

Randall House Museum, Wolfville

T HE ANTIQUE PAINTED WALLPAPER INSIDE THE RANDALL House Museum in Wolfville is not, as one might expect, pasted to the wall. Instead, a small sample of it, salvaged from its original site, hangs in a picture frame. This is because it was originally hung not in this house, but in the one formerly across the street, belonging to Thomas Andrew Strange DeWolf.

Wolfville lies at the heart of an apple-growing region in what was once known as Horton Township. The large lot on which the Thomas DeWolf house stood was acquired in the twentieth century by the Wolfville Fruit Company, which exported apples using the Dominion Atlantic rail line that ran behind the property. In 1941 the old house was threatened with demolition. A number of concerned citizens banded together to form the Wolfville Historical Society in order to save it, and for six years the society was allowed to use the building as a community museum. The fruit company offered the house to the society on condition that they move it, but this proved beyond their means. Its contents were transferred to the Randall House, across the street, which the society acquired to serve as a museum in its place. This small fragment of decorative paper, known as the DeWolf Wallpaper, that once adorned the original parlour walls, was saved, and provides a link between the two houses and the families who lived in them.

Horton Township was one of the settlements set up by Governor Lawrence to bring in Planters from New England, who would cultivate the lands left vacant after the Expulsion of the Acadians. In the 1760s three DeWolf brothers, Simeon, Nathan, and Jehiel, received grants at Grand Pré. They later settled on the small harbour of Mud Creek at the mouth of the Cornwallis River. Here, a village grew up along the Post Road west of Horton. Mud Creek soon replaced the original Horton town plot as the commercial and social centre of the township. The DeWolfs were prominent in the community, and owned much of the property there. Nathan's son Elisha became a judge, whose own son, also Elisha, became postmaster. Another son, Thomas, was engaged in the shipping business.

Village residents understandably disliked the original name. Esther Clarke Wright wrote that the judge's granddaughters "protested that they found it embarrassing at boarding school to say that they came from Mud Creek and demanded a more dignified name for the village." The change to the present name, Wolfville, took place around 1830, and was no doubt facilitated by the facts that the DeWolfs were important citizens and Elisha DeWolf Jr. was the postmaster.

Judge Elisha DeWolf was the leading man in the village in 1817, the year his son Thomas married Nancy Ratchford. Shortly after their marriage, with his father's help, Thomas built a house on the corner of Main Street and Gaspereau Avenue, near the harbour of what was then still Mud Creek. Thomas and Nancy lived there in considerable style. Among their wedding presents, so the story goes, was the wallpaper that adorned the parlour of their new house. It is said to have been the gift of Prince Edward, Duke of Kent, who was stationed in Nova Scotia for most of the last decade of the eighteenth century. The prince had been a guest of the judge during his time here, and seems to have maintained contact with the family. He would be married himself the following year, terminating his long liaison with Julie de Saint-Laurent in order to marry a German princess, with whom he ensured a legitimate successor to the British throne: their daughter, Victoria.

The wallpaper originally adorned all four walls of Thomas DeWolf's parlour. It was a type known as French scenic wallpaper, designed to create a panorama around the room rather than the repetitive patterns common to many styles. This kind of wallpaper, then called *papier peint*, was manufactured in France towards the end of the eighteenth century and for much of the nineteenth, and became very popular both in Europe in North America. It was printed with wood blocks, which were carved and their imprints superimposed one on another to portray the details of a wide variety of landscapes. Both the paper and workmanship were of high quality.

This particular pattern was called Les Jardins Français, and was designed by Antoine-Pierre Mongin of Zuber and Cie around 1820. It would therefore have been a very new and fashionable design when the young DeWolf couple came to decorate their new home. The entire panorama of a garden, with lawns, trees, and architectural elements, would have extended all around the room. The surviving fragment depicts a romantic scene between a young couple seated on a tree-shaded bench.

The Randall House, in which the wallpaper fragment now hangs, is also one of the town's heritage buildings. Dating from the early years of the nineteenth century, it once stood close to the harbour, which extended farther inland where Willow Park and its pond now lie. Its original owner, cooper Aaron Cleveland, may have also been its builder. Cleveland lived in the house from 1809 until 1812. He then sold it to Charles Randall, a carpenter and coach-maker. Randall did not live in it for long after his wife died, but rented it out for some years, then sold it to his son, Charles Denison Randall, in 1844. The house remained in the Randall family until 1927, when it was sold to Charles Patriquin. The Patriquin family restored and maintained it in its original form.

Today, the Wolfville Historical Society operates Randall House as a community museum. Among its collections is this fragment of wallpaper, both an interesting example of decorative style fashionable in former years and a symbolic link with the DeWolf family, who played an important role in the town's early development.

~ 33 ~

Thomas Chandler Haliburton's desk

1830S

Haliburton House Museum, Windsor

THOMAS CHANDLER HALIBURTON WAS BORN IN 1796 AND
brought up in Windsor, Nova Scotia. There he received a traditional classical education with the elite of Nova Scotia's society at
King's College. The oldest institution of higher learning in Canada, King's
College was established in Windsor in 1789 for the education of Anglicans
and was a stronghold of the Tory establishment to which Haliburton's

family belonged. Both his father and grandfather were lawyers and served as judges, a tradition that young Thomas would follow.

Haliburton set up a law practice in Annapolis Royal in 1820 and represented that area in the House of Assembly from 1826 to 1829. As a member, he was noted for his witty oratory. In 1829 he became a judge in the Inferior Court of Common Pleas, a position left vacant by the death of his father, William Hersey Otis Haliburton. He returned to Windsor shortly afterwards and purchased a property on a hill at the edge of the town, upon which he built a residence called Clifton. It was completed about 1836, at which time Haliburton took up residence there with his wife, Louisa, and their children. He remained there for twenty years, though Louisa died in 1841. While living there, Haliburton developed a number of commercial interests in Windsor, including stores and a gypsum quarry, and was president of the company that owned the Avon Road bridge. When the court in which he served was abolished, he was appointed to the Supreme Court of Nova Scotia.

Haliburton was also a well-known author. In 1823 he wrote *A General Description of Nova Scotia, Illustrated by a New and Correct Map*, printed at the Royal Acadian School in Halifax, followed by *An Historical and Statistical Account of Nova Scotia*, published by his friend Joseph Howe in 1829. Haliburton's best-known works are his satirical writings about Sam Slick, a fictional Yankee clockmaker. This drop-front secretary-style desk, at which these books were written, was among the original furnishings of Clifton house in Windsor. Between the drawers and pigeonholes above the writing top, a door conceals a secret compartment.

Through the voice of Sam Slick of Slickville, as narrated by his travelling companion, the Squire, Haliburton poked fun at Nova Scotia's colonial society and at American commercialism. The original sketches appeared in Howe's *The Novascotian* in 1835, where they were well received. They were then published in book form, also by Howe, the next year. *The Clockmaker; or, The Sayings and Doings of Sam Slick of Slickville*, rapidly became an international bestseller. Two additional volumes, Series 2 and 3, followed in 1838 and 1840. This work established Haliburton as a celebrated satirist and one of the most popular authors of his day, whose writings enjoyed success on both sides of the Atlantic.

Sam Slick is portrayed as an entrepreneurial American clockmaker who travelled throughout Nova Scotia, peddling his wares and recording in his Yankee idiom impressions of "human natur" as he observed it. Through Sam's philosophical observations, the author criticized the habits and attitudes of society in both British North America and the United States by making his readers laugh. Slick appears as a quick-witted and smooth-talking salesman, who, like his fellow citizens, seizes every opportunity to do business, while Nova Scotians are shown as unambitious and inward looking. In addition to amusing his audience, Haliburton introduced through Sam Slick a large number of idiomatic expressions that have passed into the English language. It is his sayings rather than his doings that have survived among readers and non-readers alike and popularized phrases like "raining cats and dogs" and "looking for a needle in a haystack."

Haliburton was a prolific author, spending many hours at this desk, and producing both serious political works and these lighter, satirical books. His writings reflected his interest in improving what he saw as the weaknesses in social and political life, and in creating a better and more prosperous society. He travelled to England from time to time and wrote about British as well as colonial life. After the success of the Clockmaker series, he went on to write *The Attaché; or Sam Slick in England*, published in 1844. He revived his hero once more in 1853 with *Sam Slick's Wise Saws and Modern Instances; or, What He Said, Did, and Invented.* Meanwhile, *The Old Judge; or, Life in a Colony*, was published in 1849 and is often considered one of his best works. However, it is *The Clockmaker* for which Haliburton is most widely known and on which his reputation as a satirist is largely based. The political writings emanating from Haliburton's desk are largely forgotten except in academic circles.

At the age of sixty, Haliburton retired from the bench to begin a new life in England, leaving his Windsor home behind him. He settled in what was then the quiet village of Isleworth, on the Thames west of

London. He served a term as Member of Parliament for Launceton in Cornwall, but became dissatisfied with Britain's political attitudes and its lack of interest in colonial development, and did not seek a second term. He continued to write, focusing his attention on British politics and idiosyncrasies, maintained his business interests, and was chairman of the Canadian Land and Immigration Company, which promoted settlement in Western Canada.

Thomas Chandler Haliburton died in 1865 and is buried in the peaceful graveyard of Isleworth Parish Church, but his desk remains in Windsor, a reminder of one of Nova Scotia's most famous authors.

～ 34 ～
Lunenburg County gold pans

C. 1860s

Ovens Natural Park, near Riverport

THE MID-NINETEENTH CENTURY SAW A FLURRY OF INTEREST in gold mining in Nova Scotia. While the province's "gold rush" was greatly overshadowed by the surge of hopeful prospectors heading westward to the Klondike and California, when gold was discovered at Mooseland in Halifax County in 1858, many people were lured to that area. Prospectors also began to look elsewhere, and a few years later, in 1861, gold was found at The Ovens in Lunenburg County.

A small museum on Ovens Natural Park site displays relics of the ensuing search for riches, including these iron pans. Prospectors used the shallow pans by swirling within them sand and gravel from the beach in search of fragments of gold. While some of the gold-bearing rock was mined on a large scale and crushed mechanically, it was the individual prospectors working with their pans who caught the imagination of later generations. To this day, visitors use pans of the same style to sift through the few remaining patches of sand on the little beach at The Ovens in the hope of finding a glimmer of gold.

In the seventeenth century the French, viewing the shoreline from the water, noted a series of caves on a peninsula on the west side of Lunenburg Bay. The caves reminded them of a row of bread ovens, so they named them *Les Fournaises*, and this is how the area was identified on early French maps. The British took over the name and translated it, making it The Ovens, which it is how it appeared on maps from the time Lunenburg was settled in 1753. Nineteen Lunenburg settlers took up 30-acre farm lots at nearby Feltzen South before 1760, but this did not include the area that is now The Ovens Natural Park. Several people subsequently owned land there, and a grant was made in 1784 to John Meisner, "of 660 acres at the Indian Ovens" as they were then known. He would have had no knowledge of any mineral wealth on his land.

The geology of the coastline at The Ovens is spectacular, with its jagged slate cliffs and deep caves. In some caves, particularly the one known as the Cannon Cave, even small incoming waves can produce a deep "boom" as they reach the inner walls. The story goes that a Mi'kmaw canoeist entered one of these caves and emerged at Annapolis Royal. The slate cliffs also contain narrow seams of quartz, some of which was found to be gold bearing. James Dowling, who made the discovery on June 13, 1861, quickly established a claim. Shortly after this discovery, John Campbell also found gold, in the sand of the little cove. Suddenly, this hitherto quiet rural area was the centre of attention, and local people rushed to see what they could find. By mid-July, every day brought more hopeful gold hunters.

Inevitably, disputes arose and the Halifax *Morning Chronicle* reported on August 3 that Joseph Howe, then provincial secretary, and other government officials sailed down from Halifax to resolve them. Other interested citizens, including William Cunard, the son of Sir Samuel, the shipping magnate, accompanied them on the voyage. William was obviously eager to become involved with the new development. The report stated that 30 × 33-ft. lots were laid out, and "Mr. Cunard, we understand, took up 70 lots, mostly in the rear, paying at the rate of five pounds each as yearly rental." It goes on to say that Cunard "returned home with the party on Sunday evening, bringing some beautiful specimens…gathered by himself." He then left Halifax again for The Ovens "with one of his own steamers fully equipped for operations."

People continued to stream in, and Mather Byles DesBrisay, in his *History of the County of Lunenburg*, describes how a small community rapidly grew up. He quotes Adolphus Gaetz: "August 31.—Upwards of 600 now at work. Shanties erected, and grocery shops and restaurants opened." Vessels even carried passengers from the United States eager for a share in the riches. Miners were employed to work the quartz seams in the cliffs and caves, and panning took place on the beach. Judge DesBrisay also tells of the high prices paid for beach lots, where, in 1861 and 1862, over one thousand ounces of gold were recovered from the sand and debris that formed as the tide eroded the cliffs. Joseph Howe was so impressed by the discovery that he wrote a detailed account of the development of the area to Lieutenant-Governor Phipps, who came to visit the site. The chief investors in The Ovens were William Cunard, John Campbell, and R. G. Fraser, who formed the Cunard Company. The lots that Cunard had leased included frontage on the beach, which proved to be the most productive area; it is known today as Cunard Cove.

Meanwhile, the cliff's quartz seams were being mined and the gold-bearing rock crushed by heavy granite wheels, which can still be seen on the site. The time and effort required to recover gold this way made it a less profitable operation than processing the sand, which yielded a higher return. No longer satisfied with panning on the beach, the Cunard Company bagged quantities of sand and brought it to Halifax for processing. But sand builds up slowly, and resources were exhausted after a few years.

The most active period of gold exploitation at The Ovens occurred between 1861 and 1864. Afterwards, production dwindled and the gold rush ended. Resurgence took place, however, in 1868, when a furnace was installed to heat quartz and sand in order to extract gold. That same year, much of the remaining sand was shipped to Wales for processing. But the boom days were over; the miners moved away, and today nothing is left of the little town that sprung up at The Ovens.

Sporadic attempts have been made from time to time to revive the gold industry in Lunenburg County, but today visitors to The Ovens enjoy the cliffs and caves for their impressive scenery. And those who pan for gold on the beach do so more for fun than in the expectation of making their fortune.

~ 35 ~

Concord stagecoach

c. 1866

Yarmouth County Museum and Archives

TWO HUNDRED YEARS AGO, WHEN MOST RESIDENTS OF NOVA
Scotia lived on or near the coast, roads fit for wheeled traffic were
almost non-existent and the normal way to travel between communities was by water. In the early nineteenth century, there were only
two reasonably good highways (by the standards of the time) crossing

the province to link Halifax with Windsor and Truro. In 1816 regular stagecoach services began to carry passengers and mail on each of those roads. Highway construction continued, and by the mid-nineteenth century a network of roads was developing. Regular stagecoach services between towns in other parts of the province soon followed. These privately operated coaches typically carried not only passengers but also mail, for which the government paid the owners. Some ran over relatively short distances, while others included an overnight stop.

This beautiful coach is one of two in the Yarmouth County Museum that were operated by Roland VanNorden to carry passengers the less than twenty kilometres between Tusket and Yarmouth in the second half of the nineteenth century. VanNorden ran a livery stable in Tusket, where travellers might hire, according to his advertisement, "Horses and Carriages, for short or long excursions, as may be required, with or without a driver, and on moderate terms." His stagecoach business began in 1865, when he acquired a small, locally made coach that carried six passengers inside and two outside, sitting beside the driver. The following year he obtained a contract to carry Her Majesty's Royal Mail.

The dirt roads that served as highways at that time were often deeply rutted, muddy in wet weather, dusty in summer, and impassable for wheeled traffic in the snowy winters, when sleighs were used. Maintenance was largely dependent on statutory labour by local residents, whose equipment was limited to picks and shovels, carts, horses, and oxen. The result was a very bumpy ride for passengers in coaches, carriages, and buggies.

After this initial period of bone-shaking travel over Nova Scotia's rough roads, VanNorden replaced his original small stagecoach with this larger, elegantly decorated vehicle, known as a Concord Coach, made in Concord, New Hampshire, by the Abbot-Downing Company between 1826 and 1899. This company made a wide range of coaches and carriages, but the Concord Coach was famous all over North America for its superior comfort. Instead of having a steel sprung suspension, the body of the coach was slung on heavy leather straps, which greatly reduced the jolting impact on the passengers from the rough dirt roads over which they travelled. The vehicles were custom-made of high-quality materials, and tastefully decorated.

This version of the Concord Coach purchased by VanNorden could carry nine passengers inside: three on each bench, and three on a seat across the middle. As many as six more could ride outside, beside the coachman or perched on a seat at the front of the roof. Baggage was stowed on top, and mail was carried on a rack at the back of the coach or between the driver's feet. Weighing 2,500 pounds, the coach was pulled by four, or even six horses. The finely painted decoration includes a pretty rural scene on the door and the names Yarmouth and Tusket, the towns the coach served, across the top.

Though the distance on the old road from Tusket to Yarmouth was less than twenty kilometres, the journey took about an hour if all went well. VanNorden's advertisement includes a schedule: Every day except Sunday,

> [his] easy, comfortable covered COACH...will leave the Post Office, in Tusket, at 9 A.M., arrive in Yarmouth about 10, and leave there, from the Coach office at Chas. E. Clements', near Rogers' Stable, at 4 P.M. Every attention will be paid to the comfort and convenience of passengers, and to parcels and commissions, when regularly booked at the Post Office, in Tusket, and C. E. Clements, in Yarmouth.

Later, VanNorden extended his stagecoach route as far as Pubnico. His son, William, continued the service and maintained it until 1897, when this once state-of-the art vehicle became obsolete. The coming of the railway to southwest Nova Scotia at the end of the nineteenth century put an end to the days of stagecoaches, but this fine example has survived, a symbol of a bygone era of public transportation over the province's early roads.

~ 36 ~

Ship's bell, HMCS *Niobe*

1897

Maritime Command Museum, Halifax

THIS SHIP'S BELL MARKS A TURNING POINT IN CANADA'S naval history.

Halifax was established in 1749 in response to the need for a strong British military and naval presence on the North Atlantic coast to counteract the French Fortress of Louisbourg. In 1758 the British

Admiralty, under the supervision of Captain James Cook, began construction of a naval station just north of the main settlement. The Royal Naval Dockyard was officially commissioned the following year. Ships from Halifax served in the Seven Years' War and the American Revolutionary War, the War of 1812, and subsequent conflicts. Except for a brief period after 1819, when the British government transferred most naval activities to the other North Atlantic station, at Bermuda, the dockyard continued to expand.

For much of the nineteenth century the Royal Naval Dockyard was a self-contained community, with residential and recreational facilities, wharves, stores, a mast pond, and other facilities for maintaining and refitting, first sailing vessels and later ironclad warships. There was also a hospital as well as a cemetery for officers and men of the Royal Navy. The establishment was under the command of the British admiral, who was an important personage in Halifax society, and by 1819, when Edward Griffith was serving as admiral, the fine stone residence known as Admiralty House had been completed for his use.

For many years after Confederation, Canada did not have its own navy and depended on Britain for its sea defences. Halifax's dockyard remained one of the two naval stations in the North Atlantic maintained by the British Admiralty. But in 1906 Britain abandoned its base in Halifax, and as Thomas Raddall wrote in *Halifax, Warden of the North*, "The Dockyard became a place of rust and ghosts. Admiralty House was closed and its furniture sold." Today, Admiralty House is a national historic site and home to the Maritime Command Museum. Standing on the grounds of the former Naval Dockyard, now Canadian Forces Base Stadacona, the museum's collections tell the story of the Royal Canadian Navy. Included is this ship's bell, from the first vessel to be commissioned for the RCN's East Coast fleet.

The Royal Navy left Halifax in 1906, when the British government decided to make Bermuda its only North Atlantic naval station. The Canadian Government, which had already been considering establishing a navy of its own, took over the dockyard site. After some controversy,

Sir Wilfred Laurier's government passed legislation in 1910, establishing what was initially called the Naval Service of Canada. The following year, the service would be re-named the Royal Canadian Navy. It would work with and support the Royal Navy. Canada owned no naval vessels, so a cruiser was obtained from the British.

HMS *Niobe* sailed into Halifax Harbour on October 21, 1910, soon to become HMCS *Niobe*, the Canadian Navy's first vessel on the Atlantic coast. Built at the Vickers shipyards in Barrow-in-Furness, northern England, *Niobe* was launched in 1897 and commissioned in 1898—the date on the bell. (Standard equipment on a ship, the bell was struck one to eight times at half-hourly intervals during the four-hour watches, or periods of duty, into which a seaman's life was divided.) HMCS *Niobe* served with the Royal Navy's Channel Squadron before being sent to Gibraltar to escort troopships to South Africa during the Boer War. Her participation earned her crew members the South Africa Medal. After the war she returned to the Channel Squadron, and her peacetime activities took her as far as Colombo, in what is now Sri Lanka. Her first transatlantic voyage brought her to Halifax.

Niobe's captain was W. G. MacDonald, a Canadian who had served in the Royal Navy. His immediate task was to train recruits for Canada's own navy, and in 1911 a college for naval officers was established in Halifax, with HMCS *Niobe* as a training vessel. *Niobe* sustained some damage by running aground near Yarmouth later that year, but after repairs she resumed her training duties until the outbreak of the First World War. Her first task, under the command of Captain R. G. Corbett, RN, was to escort troops of the Royal Canadian Regiment to Bermuda for garrison duty. Thereafter she worked with Royal Navy ships, carrying out patrol, convoy, and blockade duties along the Atlantic coast. By the end of 1915 *Niobe* was beginning to show her age and was reassigned to Halifax as a depot ship until the end of the war.

Her adventures were not over, however. In wartime, the spacious Bedford Basin was an ideal spot for assembling the convoys of ships carrying troops and supplies to Britain under naval escort. There was heavy traffic at that time between the basin and Halifax Harbour. On December 6, 1917, as *Niobe* lay in her berth at the dockyard, the catastrophic collision between the French munitions ship *Mont Blanc* and the Norwegian *Imo* took place in The Narrows, precipitating the Halifax Explosion. Foreseeing the impending disaster, the French crew abandoned ship, leaving the *Mont Blanc* adrift in the harbour. The *Niobe*'s bo's'n and six of her crew were dispatched, along with crews from other vessels, in an attempt to extinguish the fire and tow the burning vessel away from shore. These men lost their lives when the flames reached the highly explosive cargo and the *Mont Blanc* blew up.

The huge explosion caused devastation to large areas of Halifax's North End and across the harbour in Dartmouth. Canada's first naval vessel was also damaged and, already an old ship, *Niobe* served for only a few more years as a depot ship before being decommissioned in 1920. She was sold for scrap and broken up in Philadelphia in 1922. Her bell, along with other memorabilia from the ship, is now displayed in Admiralty House. Additional souvenirs can be found in the Maritime Museum of the Atlantic.

The Canadian Navy was a relatively small force at the outset of the Second World War, but an urgent shipbuilding programme rapidly increased its numbers with corvettes and minesweepers, and Canadian sailors played a distinguished role in the Battle of the Atlantic. Since 1945 the dockyard has been modernized and most of the original buildings replaced. Admiralty House survives as a reminder of the old dockyard, and this bell from HMS *Niobe* symbolizes the birth of our navy.

～ 37 ～

LaHave Island sea chest

C. 1900

LaHave Islands Marine Museum, Bell Island

AT THE MOUTH OF THE LaHAVE RIVER IS A GROUP OF ISLANDS
that have been home to many generations of seamen since British
settlement began in the area towards the end of the eighteenth
century. While most residents lived on Bell and Bush Islands, the two
largest, one or two families made their homes on the smaller LaHave
islands, and much of Cape LaHave Island was designated as common

land where locals could cut hay or pasture their animals. By the end of the nineteenth century, Judge DesBrisay estimated that sixty-one families lived on the LaHave Islands. During that time, Bell and Bush Islands were home to lively fishing communities with their own schools and churches. Whether they worked on the inshore fishing boats, sailed schooners to the Banks, or crewed on trading vessels bound for the West Indies, the men from the islands made their lives on the sea from an early age.

The island children attended one of the two schools on Bush and Bell Islands. Children from the smaller islands came across by boat in spring and fall, and in winter sometimes walked to school over the ice. The one-room schools went up to grade nine, though not all the children stayed in school until they were fourteen. A few went on to attend high school on the mainland, but most of the boys joined their fathers and neighbours and became fishermen. The LaHave Islanders depended on the sea for their living and often worked on fishing vessels all their lives.

The fishing industry along the coast of Nova Scotia dates back to when European vessels—British, French, Spanish, Portuguese, and Basque— crossed the Atlantic every summer in search of cod. Nicolas Denys and others had started up a few year-round French fishing settlements in the seventeenth century, but the LaHave fishery was not developed until many years after the British gained control of Nova Scotia in 1713. The Foreign Protestant settlers of Lunenburg Township were farmers, not fishermen, and it was only later in the eighteenth century, when land was granted in New Dublin Township on the west side of the LaHave, that fishing became established there. As the population spread to the LaHave Islands, fishing became a way of life.

The owner of this sea chest, which is now in the LaHave Islands Marine Museum on Bell Island, is known to the museum only as "Eddie." He was no more than eleven years old when he first went to sea, probably in the late nineteenth or early twentieth century. Eddie was young to go to sea. We don't know if it was his desire for adventure, a loathing for the restrictions of school, or family hardship that took him away from home at such an early age. Nor do we know whether he went with an older relative who was also a crew member, or if he was taken on by a local sea captain who could use a boy for odd jobs around his vessel.

The crew's quarters, where Eddie would have lived, were in the bow of the ship and consisted of bunks along the sides and a table with benches in the centre, and no other seating. Here the men slept, ate, and played cards or swapped stories. There was little space for personal property, but each crew member had his sea chest, in which he stowed his spare clothing and perhaps a few personal items for the voyage. Typically, these wooden chests had one or two built-in compartments, in which smaller things—a book, a pack of cards, a photo or a souvenir from a loved one—could be kept separately.

Eddie's chest is interestingly decorated. As well as his name, which stands out in white on the blue-painted front, there is inside the lid a primitive but nicely rendered painting of a fully rigged, two-masted schooner, perhaps representing the vessel on which Eddie sailed. Details such as the white bow, waves, and reflections of the clouds in the water show the care with which the painting was done. What may be two whales appear: one below the schooner, one ahead of it. A white shoreline lies in the distance and a red lighthouse stands near a faint image of a house, with perhaps a red barn beyond. The original lighthouse on Cross Island at the entrance to Lunenburg Harbour was painted red—did the anonymous artist have this in mind? We don't know who decorated this chest, but it is a fine reminder of the days when wooden fishing schooners like the one shown here left the LaHave River for the Grand Banks off southern Newfoundland, and of their crew members, many of whom came from the LaHave Islands.

Today, a road and bridge carry traffic to Bell and Bush Islands. The schools have closed. A few fishing boats can still be seen in the little island harbour, but sailing ships have given way to newer, diesel-powered vessels. Many of the original families have been replaced by cottage owners and summer visitors. And the old Methodist church, later a United church, has become home to the Marine Museum, where this lovely old sea chest is preserved.

~ 38 ~

Victorian horseless carriage

1900

Museum of Industry, Stellarton

D URING THE NINETEENTH CENTURY, NOVA SCOTIA'S ROADS
developed from a series of rough tracks between communities—most passable only on foot or horseback—to
what became the framework for today's highway system. Wheeled
traffic at this time consisted of privately owned carriages, buggies,
and farm wagons, and commercially operated stagecoach services.
The *Victorian* carriage on display at Stellarton's Museum of Industry

looks, at first glance, like any other conveyance of its day, as if waiting for a horse to be brought from the stable to pull it. But it lacks the shafts necessary to attach a horse, and it is in fact self-propelled. The *Victorian* was built in Nova Scotia at the very end of the century by John MacArthur, of Hopewell, Pictou County. Completed in 1900, it was the first gasoline-powered motor car to be built in the Maritimes, and the first of a series of car-making initiatives in Nova Scotia.

At the turn of the century, the concept of gasoline-powered automobiles was beginning to grip the imagination of the Western world. Experimental steam-operated vehicles had been devised in the late eighteenth century and further developed in the nineteenth, but steam power eventually proved more popular for railway locomotives than for highway use. When gasoline and diesel internal combustion engines were invented in Germany towards the end of the nineteenth century, they rapidly became the more popular means of propulsion.

John MacArthur was a furniture manufacturer whose entrepreneurial interests were obviously not limited to tables and chairs: he pioneered automobile manufacture in Nova Scotia. To construct the *Victorian*, he purchased its two-cylinder engine, probably of German manufacture, in New York, and obtained the plans for the body design from a Massachusetts carriage maker. The *Victorian*'s frame is made of one-inch iron pipes, with a wooden body, a single leather-upholstered seat, and four thirty-inch wooden wheels. It represents an experimental, transitional stage between a horse-drawn vehicle and a modern automobile. The description provided by the Museum of Industry information sheet outlines some of the *Victorian*'s technical specifications:

> The engine, mounted "underhind" the seat, operated a jackshaft, incorporating a cone clutch, a band-type brake, and an open differential. Final drive was by the flat belts from each end of the jackshaft to the rear wheels. The "carburetor" consisted of another piece of one-inch pipe, in which dripping gasoline was vaporized by in-rushing air. The radiator consisted of an

ordinary tank with 2-inch pipes for air passage. Steering was by tiller.

When MacArthur's "horseless carriage" first took to the road in 1900, the belt drive performed poorly and was soon replaced by a sprocket drive and chain, like that of a bicycle. The *Victorian* was still a disappointment, however, only being capable of speeds up to eight kilometres per hour on the flat, and requiring a push to go uphill. As a result, the carriage was never developed commercially. Still, it remains a landmark in industrial history as Nova Scotia's first locally made car, though not the last.

While Nova Scotia was never destined to rival Detroit, commercial car manufacture began here in 1908, when brothers Daniel and John McKay took over the Nova Scotia Carriage Company in Kentville, and adapted it for automobile production as the Nova Scotia Carriage and Motor Company. In 1910 the McKay brothers produced their first cars. With the help of a man called Archie Pelton, who taught himself the technical details; his brother, Roy Pelton, and a man named Young who were cabinetmakers; and a third McKay brother who was a blacksmith, the McKay car was developed. Once again, the engines were imported from the United States, while the bodies were made in Nova Scotia. However, the design was no longer an adaptation of the traditional carriage, but more closely resembled a modern vehicle with the motor at the front.

The locally made McKay car provided an alternative to luxury American imports. The Museum of Industry displays a 1912 seven-seater touring model, with a 4-cylinder, 40-horsepower engine, a steering wheel, and rubber tires. Its licence plate identifies it as the 170th car to be registered in the province. Found in pieces in a barn in the 1970s, it was restored by the Pictou County Antique Car Club. This model was one of the last to be made in Kentville, as the McKays were persuaded to move the business to Amherst that same year. By 1913 the McKay car was back in production, but the expense of the new building combined with an economic downturn proved disastrous, and the plant closed in 1914.

A third attempt at car manufacturing in Nova Scotia was launched in the 1960s, when the Swedish Volvo Company established an assembly plant in an old Dartmouth sugar refinery, as a result of an initiative sponsored by a provincial crown corporation, Industrial Estates Ltd., to encourage industrial development. Parts were brought in by ship from Sweden and assembled in the Dartmouth plant for distribution in North America. The model on display in the museum is the Volvo Canadian, the first car to come off the Dartmouth assembly line in 1963. Prince Bertil of Sweden attended its ceremonial completion and formally tightened the last screw. The car was given to the provincial minister of Trade and Industry, who used it for some time before donating it to the Nova Scotia Museum in 1967.

Sales soon increased as the popularity of the Volvo Canadian grew. The Volvo plant moved to Halifax and in 1967 to the Bayers Lake Industrial Park, where two hundred workers were employed and eight thousand cars assembled in a year. Production peaked in 1975, and was again high in the mid-1980s. But by 1998, the company's overall production capacity was exceeding demand, and the Nova Scotia plant was closed. This ended the province's car manufacturing history, which had begun with the old *Victorian* and lasted for nearly a century.

～ 39 ～

No. 10 Reserve Mine bull wheel

C. 1905

Cape Breton Miners Museum, Glace Bay

THIS BULL WHEEL IS REPRESENTATIVE OF THE ERA OF MECH-
anized coal mining in the early twentieth century. During this
time, these wheels stood at pitheads all over the Sydney coalfield.
Turned by an engine on the surface, they transmitted power to machinery
underground by means of an endless cable. Today the bull wheel stands

against the sky as a symbol of the industry on which the community of Glace Bay was built.

Used from 1905 to 1942 at Reserve's No. 10 Mine, this massive bull wheel is part of the outdoor display of the Cape Breton Miners Museum, located at the previous site of Ocean Deeps Colliery in Glace Bay. The town stands beside the bay of the same name, originally identified by the French as Baie de Glace. Through exhibits and tours of the mine shaft, the museum tells the story of coal formation in prehistoric times, and of the work involved in extracting it from this and other mines in the Sydney Coalfield. The interior display of miners' equipment includes many relics of Glace Bay's once flourishing coal-mining industry, including a smaller replica of the wheel.

Although Cape Breton's most productive years were those between the mid-nineteenth and mid-twentieth centuries, the story of coal mining in the area goes back much farther. Exposed coal seams in the cliffs along the shore of Cape Breton, from the Mira to Inverness, were visible to sailors travelling along the coast hundreds of years ago. Nicolas Denys wrote in his *Description and Natural History of Acadia*, first published in 1672, "one comes to the Riviere des Espagnols [Sydney Harbour], at whose entrance ships can anchor in safety. There is a hill of very good coal four leagues farther within the river." Denys had seen only a small portion of the Sydney Coalfield.

In the early eighteenth century the French established the first mine at nearby Morien Bay to supply coal to their fortress at Louisbourg. Initially, coal was simply hacked out of the cliff face or from shallow surface pits on land with picks and crowbars, and then shovelled into containers for transport. Because of its high gas content, coal was a fire hazard. During the French regime it was used only locally, as French authorities forbade its transportation across the Atlantic in the wooden vessels of the day. A British map from the early 1760s identifies coal seams in many places along this coast, including one that was burning. This is probably the mine at Table Head mentioned by Carole MacDonald in her *Historic Glace Bay* as having been set on fire by disgruntled French miners in

1752, and which continued to burn for years afterwards.

Mining in Cape Breton was actually forbidden by the British authorities in the second half of the eighteenth century; it was not resumed until the London-based General Mining Association acquired mineral rights in Cape Breton and opened a mine at North Sydney in 1830. In Glace Bay, mining began in the second half of the nineteenth century when the GMA no longer held the monopoly. The first mine was the Hub Shaft, opened in 1861 by the Glace Bay Mining Company. Several other mines followed in the 1860s, but a recession in the 1870s reduced demand for coal.

Mining resumed on a large scale in Glace Bay only after 1893, with the establishment of the Dominion Coal Company (later DOSCO). Operating eleven mines in the area, it attracted an influx of immigrant workers of many nationalities who formed small settlements clustered around the pitheads. Soon, the increasing population brought about the amalgamation of the communities that had grown up around the various mines into the present town of Glace Bay, which was incorporated in 1901. DOSCO would operate mines there until 1967.

The Miners Museum demonstrates how hard and dangerous the miners' work was as they hacked at the narrow seams of coal, often crouching in the cramped space or lying prone. As the mines expanded, the seams often ran many hundreds of metres deep underground and some kilometres out to sea. Initially men worked with picks at the coal face, loading the coal onto cars which, for many years, were drawn on rails towards the surface by sturdy pit ponies. As time went on, mechanical cutters replaced picks for retrieving coal, motors replaced the ponies for moving coal cars, and cables from the bull wheels operated the underground machinery.

Miners spent the entire workday underground. The pay was low and the work was arduous. Before legislation was passed prohibiting child labour, mines often employed young boys because they could crawl into spaces too small for adult men. (Sons often accompanied their fathers to the pit, and went on to work there for the rest of their lives.) Fire from methane gas and coal dust was a constant hazard and could cause deadly explosions. The Davy safety lamp, invented in 1815, was originally used in the mines to minimize the risk of an exposed flame igniting the gas. Later, miners wore helmets with battery-operated headlamps. Another danger was the chance of a rock-fall that could crush workers or block their way to the surface. Wooden, and later steel, posts were installed to support the top of the seam and reduce this risk.

Over the years, safety standards improved in the mines. Telephones were installed for communication, along with methane monitors and ventilation. Nevertheless, there were accidents from time to time. One of the last was an explosion at the No. 26 Colliery, which caused the death of twelve men in March 1979. By then, with coal sales declining, DOSCO had ceased to operate the remaining mines, which were taken over in 1967 by the Cape Breton Development Corporation. The last mine closed in the 1980s, bringing to an end the long history of coal in Glace Bay.

Though pithead machinery is no longer a common feature of the area, this massive wheel is a reminder of the former importance of the coal-mining industry, which for many years was the mainstay of Cape Breton's economy.

～ 40 ～

Sambro Island lighthouse first-order Fresnel lens

1906

Maritime Museum of the Atlantic, Halifax

THIS HUGE, 2.8 METRE-HIGH AND 1.76 METRE-WIDE FRESNEL lens from Sambro Island lighthouse stands just inside the Maritime Museum of the Atlantic on the Halifax waterfront. One of the museum's most striking artefacts, it links land and sea and represents an important era of development in Nova Scotia's lighthouses.

The history of lighthouses goes back a long way. Completed in 280 BC, the *Pharos* (Greek for "lighthouse")—considered one of the seven wonders of the ancient world—guided navigators into the port of Alexandria and continued to do so until its destruction by an earthquake in the fourteenth century. The French at Louisbourg completed the first lighthouse in what is now Canada in 1734, and in 1758 the British established the first on the Nova Scotia mainland, the Sambro Island light at the entrance to Halifax Harbour.

By this time, Cape Sambro, known to Champlain as Cap Sesambre, had been a landmark for navigators along the coast of Nova Scotia for over 150 years. After Halifax was established in 1749 as a British naval base and the administrative and commercial centre of Nova Scotia, an increasing number of both military and commercial vessels used the harbour—along with the fishing boats that sheltered there. The coast is rocky and treacherous, and as early as 1752 it was thought desirable to establish a lighthouse at the Halifax Harbour entrance to guide this traffic safely into port. After initial attempts at funding failed, an Act of the Assembly was passed in October 1758 authorizing the work. It would be financed from duties on liquor and a tax on ships entering the harbour. Construction began immediately, and before the end of the year the building was almost completed and a temporary light installed. By the following spring, the Sambro Island lighthouse was operational.

The stone-built lighthouse was originally almost twenty metres high. It showed a white, fixed light without reflectors that was smoky and inefficient, and not always well maintained—the job of lighthouse keeper was then a patronage appointment in the gift of the governor. Later, lamps with flues, used to carry away smoke, improved visibility, and over the years the light became increasingly efficient and the keepers more professional, as employees of the federal government. In 1834 a commission recommended that the multi-paned lantern at the top of the Sambro Island lighthouse tower be replaced, but this was not done until 1864. That year, an iron-framed lantern with plate glass panes was installed along with reflecting mirrors, which focused the lamp's rays and increased its range. Over the years the lamp was fuelled by seal oil, then by whale oil, kerosene, and finally acetylene.

A major improvement took place in 1906: an extra 7 metres were added to the lighthouse structure, and this first-order Fresnel lens, made in France, replaced the reflector lamp. This further increased the light's range of visibility. Developed for lighthouse use in 1823 by Augustin-Jean Fresnel, compact multi-faceted lenses were made by grinding concentric grooves in crystal glass, creating prisms that reproduced the curvature of a conventional convex lens while reducing its thickness. This technique allows the installation of a much stronger lens in the limited space of a lighthouse lantern. Fresnel lenses are classified in a variety of "orders" depending on their size and focal length. This first-order lens, standing 2.8 metres high, is one of the largest. It has four faces, each with twelve prisms set in a bronze frame.

In 1966 Sambro Island light's large lens was replaced by the electric-powered Directional Code Beacon (DCB). The DCB too has a Fresnel-type lens, moulded rather than cut, and is much smaller and less powerful. But a strong, one-thousand-watt bulb compensated for this, remaining visible for many kilometres. It required little maintenance and ran almost continuously until 2008, when Sambro's most recent light, run on solar power, was installed after heavy seas broke the electricity cable from the mainland to the island.

Over the years, Nova Scotia's lighthouses have seen many changes. Originally, each housed a resident keeper whose job it was to maintain the lamp and to sound a manually operated foghorn when required. During the second half of the twentieth century, many of the province's lighthouses were automated and then decommissioned, as the government believed that ships with modern radar and GPS equipment no longer needed their guiding light. Some lighthouses have been taken over and cared for by local communities, but the fate of others, including Sambro Island light, is uncertain. Once landmarks for travellers both by land and sea, their cause has been taken up by the Lighthouse Preservation Society, which strives to maintain their continued presence on our coasts. This lens is part of their long history.

$\sim$ 41 $\sim$

Silver Dart propeller

1909

Alexander Graham Bell Museum, Baddeck

ONE ARTEFACT CANNOT DO JUSTICE TO THE INVENTIVE spirit of Alexander Graham Bell. His name is associated with important developments in several fields of scientific technology and his wide-ranging interests were in many ways similar to those of Leonardo da Vinci. But while da Vinci's ideas were far ahead of those of his contemporaries, Bell was a man of his time. He studied contemporary problems that other people were also exploring. One of the fields in which Bell carried out many experiments was aerodynamics, and his work resulted in the successful launching of the Silver Dart, the first airplane to fly in Canada. This propeller, displayed at the Alexander Graham Bell Museum in Baddeck, comes from the original plane, of which a splendid replica now hangs in the museum. It was just one of many products of Bell's versatile genius.

Alexander Graham Bell was born in Edinburgh in 1847. His father, like other members of his family, taught elocution and speech therapy. His mother had become deaf, and Bell Senior specialized in methods of communication with the hearing impaired, including lip-reading, a system of sign language, and what he called "visible speech," written symbols representing sound. Young Alexander followed in his father's footsteps and became his assistant, later working as a teacher. He became interested in the physics of both sound and electricity, and attended Edinburgh and later London University. As a student, he created a telegraph system connecting his room and that of a friend, a portent of his later fame as a developer of the telephone.

Partly on account of Alexander's precarious health, the Bell family moved to Canada in 1870 and settled on a farm near Brantford, Ontario. Here, Alexander set up a workshop where he continued his experiments with the electrical transmission of sound. After a short stay in Boston in 1871, he moved there the following year to work as a teacher of the deaf, returning to Canada in summertime. Among his students was Helen Keller, the blind deaf-mute whom he helped learn to communicate and lead a productive and less isolated life. Bell gradually devoted more and more time to scientific experiment, until one of his few remaining hearing-impaired students was Mabel Hubbard, whom he married in 1877.

At this time the telegraph system for written messages was developing rapidly, but Bell continued to pursue experiments with transmission of sound in competition with a man called Elisha Gray, who filed a patent application at about the same time as Bell. Shortly afterwards, in March 1876, Bell succeeded in transmitting a voice message to his assistant in the next room. That summer, Bell demonstrated that a spoken message from Brantford could be heard at Bell's childhood summer home, six kilometres away, by means of wires connecting the two places. From this beginning, the telephone system was developed and improved until it grew into the sophisticated devices that are used worldwide today. The phone company that Bell established in North America still bears his name.

Bell's interests were far-reaching, and as well as registering patents for telephone and telegraph devices, he devised a photophone that used light waves to transmit sound, and a phonograph for playing sound recordings. He also developed a metal detector, an iron lung, and an early form of air conditioning, studied genetics to breed sheep, and experimented with the desalinizing of water.

In the late 1880s Alexander and Mabel Bell built a summer home outside Baddeck. He named it Beinn Bhreagh (Gaelic for "beautiful mountain"). Here, in 1908, with his assistant, Frederick W. (Casey) Baldwin, and with Mabel's encouragement, Bell began to develop hydrofoils. At that time a new concept in naval construction, hydrofoil vessels operate with blades that lift them higher in the water as their speed increases, thus reducing the water's resistance. Their first experimental models culminated in the successful launching of the HD4, a sixty-foot-long vessel with two sets of hydrofoil blades, completed just before the First World War. After the war, work resumed, and in 1919, powered by US Navy engines, the HD4 achieved a world marine-speed record of 114.04 kilometres per hour.

Bell had begun to experiment with aerodynamics in the 1890s, constructing and flying tetrahedral kites with a view to developing a flying machine. In 1907, shortly after the Wright brothers made their first successful flight, Bell established the Aerial Experiment Association (AEA) at Baddeck with financial backing from his wife, and in partnership with two Americans and two Canadians, Casey Baldwin and J. A. D. McCurdy. The following year, their first aircraft, the Red Wing, took off from Hammondsport, New York, with Baldwin at the controls. It was the first public flight by a Canadian. Two more aircraft, modified and improved versions of the first, were later developed.

The lessons learned from these early experiments were incorporated into the Silver Dart, the final product of the AEA. In comparison with modern aircraft, it was incredibly flimsy. Its frame was made of steel tubing and bamboo, wire, and wood, and the wings were covered in the fabric used for hot-air balloons. This surviving propeller was carved out of a block of wood. The Silver Dart first took flight over the frozen Bras D'Or Lake, on February 23, 1909. Piloted by McCurdy, the plane flew low over the lake for a distance of 1 kilometre, at about 65 kilometres per hour. It made several more flights over a greater distance, but ran into trouble while McCurdy was demonstrating it for the military at Petawawa, Ontario, in August 1909. The sandy runway made taking off and landing difficult, and the Silver Dart crashed when a wheel became stuck on landing.

After the AEA was dissolved, McCurdy and Baldwin obtained the Canadian patent rights to the Silver Dart's design and formed a new company to build more versions of the plane. In the 1950s, to celebrate the fiftieth anniversary of the Silver Dart's maiden flight, members of the Royal Canadian Air Force built a replica. After many years at the Canadian Aviation and Space Museum in Ottawa, it is now on view in Baddeck, along with this propeller from the original plane.

~ 42 ~

Africville altar,
Seaview African
United Baptist Church

C. 1916

Africville Museum, Halifax

THIS PIECE OF FURNITURE, GIVEN PRIDE OF PLACE IN THE
Africville Museum, was the focal point of a church that no longer
exists in a community that no longer exists, except in the hearts
and minds of those who once lived there. Of all the artefacts celebrating

Black history in Nova Scotia, perhaps none is as poignant as this, identified by the curator of the Africville Museum as the altar from the Seaview African United Baptist Church. It is a type of lectern, from which the scriptures were read and church services conducted. It is all that remains of the church that was once the centre of a distinct community.

Africville was established in the 1840s by a group of African Nova Scotians from Hammonds Plains looking for a home closer to Halifax in order to work in the city. William Brown, William Arnold, Eppy Carvery, Henry Hill, and Bennett Fletcher purchased the land along Campbell Road that would become Africville, and their families formed the core of the new community. Africville was isolated from the rest of Halifax, separated at first by open countryside and then by industrial development and the railway. The residents were originally self-sufficient, with people working in Halifax, mostly as labourers or domestic servants, growing small gardens in the rocky soil, keeping a few pigs or goats, and catching fish in the Bedford Basin.

The people of Africville were predominantly Baptists, and religion was important to them. The Campbell Road Baptist Church, a branch of the African Baptist Association built in 1849, was central to community life. Baptisms took place in the Bedford Basin, and the Easter sunrise service was a well-loved tradition. It began as early as 4 or 5 A.M. and the prayers, preaching, and singing lasted until noon, when the baptisms were performed. The community was too small to employ a permanent minister, however, and much of its leadership was left in the hands of deacons and elders. Up until Africville's destruction and the relocation of its residents in the mid-1960s, the church remained the communal hub for a solid core of established families. Even people who did not attend regularly came to special events like the sunrise service. The church was a social meeting place, the centre for cultural activities and community meetings. It was also the site of the community's first school, until 1883 when a city school was built. The original church building was dismantled after the construction of a railway line close by caused the structure to deteriorate, and was replaced in 1916 by a new building on land leased from the city. It was then known as the Seaview African United Baptist Church and served the community for fifty years.

Africville was originally a viable community, but during the twentieth century, particularly after the First World War, an influx of transients—indigent Blacks and poor Whites—contributed to its gradual decline into a severely disadvantaged area, one considered a slum by outsiders. This problem was greatly exacerbated by the refusal of city authorities to provide mains water, sewer services, adequate street lighting, paved roads, public transport, or proper policing even though Africville residents paid taxes. Pollution destroyed the fishing in the basin, the community was cut in two by railway lines—and surrounded by industrial development and an abattoir—and in the 1950s Halifax established a city dump on Africville's doorstep. Under these conditions, bootlegging, illegal drinking establishments, and other illicit activities sprang up, to the dismay of older residents who maintained a respectable lifestyle. The unemployed survived by salvaging saleable material from the dump. After the school closed in 1953, Africville children were bussed to other city schools, but met with discrimination; attendance declined.

The mid-twentieth century was a period of urban renewal in many cities. During this time, Halifax saw Africville both as a social problem to be dealt with and as a potential site for further industrial development. As early as 1945, a civic planning committee, without consulting its residents, proposed the removal of Africville. Although nothing was done at the time, Africville residents again requested the city provide them with the same services other taxpayers received in an effort to improve their living conditions. Their appeals were ignored, and in 1961 the question of relocation came up again. By now, disheartened residents had little incentive to improve their properties, even if they were able to do so.

This time the city pushed ahead with plans for relocation, which took place in the mid-1960s. A committee with some Black members was appointed to look after the interests of the Africville residents, but very little consultation took place. Meetings held in the church were often poorly attended. Some residents were resigned or even eager to move, while many others resisted the idea. Gradually, under threat of expropriation, most Africville residents were persuaded to sell their property with the promise of assistance relocating into social housing or other accommodations. But negotiations were complicated. While some people held title to their land, others had inherited property without formal registration of ownership, or were squatters, so calculation of compensation was difficult.

Up until this point, many Africville residents felt they had been treated unfairly, but their resentment was nothing compared to that engendered by the actual move. City trucks transferred people's belongings, and some complained that garbage trucks had been used. Immediately after a house was vacated, it was torn down, and soon there was nothing left of Africville. When the church was bulldozed during the night, only the vigilance of one resident saved its altar from destruction.

The Africville site was not developed for industrial use. Instead, Seaview Park was established there in 1985 as a memorial to the former community. In 1996 the area was designated a national historic site, and in 2010 the Africville Genealogy Society finally received an apology from the Halifax Regional Municipality for the destruction of their community. The society also received funding for a replica of the church. It opened in 2012 as Africville Museum, an appropriate home for this treasure.

~ 43 ~

Doll carriage

LATE 1930S

Canadian Museum of Immigration at Pier 21, Halifax

THE MUSEUM AT PIER 21 IN HALIFAX IS ESTABLISHED IN WHAT was once the immigration shed for the ocean terminal, where over the years many immigrants first set foot on Canadian soil. From here, most took trains for western cities or rural areas, where they hoped to find work or set up a business. As many as 1 million newcomers passed through this area between 1928 and 1971.

New Canadians arrived from a variety of places and economic backgrounds. Some were fleeing persecution or poverty in their homelands in Germany or Eastern Europe. At the beginning of the Second World War, child evacuees arrived; they had been sent away from the imminent dangers of wartime Britain to live with Canadian families for the duration of hostilities. Later, war brides came to join their Canadian husbands, who had married them while serving overseas. Many people also came to Canada from devastated Europe after the war in search of new beginnings. Some came, as people have done since the seventeenth century, simply looking for greater opportunities than they had found in their birthplace.

These newcomers included single, young people with a spirit of adventure looking to make their fortune, or at least a better living than they enjoyed at home, as well as middle-class couples with families who hoped to establish themselves in this country and provide their children with a comfortable home and good prospects for the future. Some immigrants were desperately poor, bringing with them little more than the clothes on their backs and a suitcase, provided by the immigration agents, with a few meagre possessions. One man came with nothing in his suitcase but the toothbrush that had been issued to him. What these immigrants offered Canada was a willingness to work hard wherever they could find employment, on farms, in mines, or anywhere manual labour was needed. Some spoke little or no English or French and required the help of interpreters to navigate the customs and immigration procedures. There were also better-off families who could afford to bring with them possessions that would help them to feel at home in their new surroundings. Among these items was this doll carriage, belonging to an eight-year-old girl —we'll call her Mary, though that was not her name—who arrived from England after the Second World War.

Her family lived in Kent, and had run a café until shortly before they left, like so many people in postwar Britain, to seek broader horizons. Mary's mother had a sister in Canada, so that was their destination. Immigration to Canada was a fairly easy process for British citizens at that time. After applying to Canada House in London, completing the immigration requirements, and selling their house, her family sailed from Southampton on the Cunard liner *Aquitania* on September 13, 1949.

Before she left, Mary said farewell to her schoolmates and packed up her prized possessions. Her father made a wooden crate for her doll carriage, a replica of the pram used by Princess (now Queen) Elizabeth in the late 1930s. Passed down to her from an older cousin, it was a fashionable design, chosen by well-to-do families with nannies, and imitated in cheaper versions by the rest of the population. Into the crate Mary stuffed her favourite toys, dolls, and books. She also brought with her wartime memories of rationing, gas masks, and air raid shelters. In an interview at Pier 21, she recalled a happier event: "A big parade [came] through town because the war was over...the town had garden parties all down the streets...you sit there and have ice cream and Jell-O and all that. And my mom made me a dress out of a Union Jack flag for the occasion."

Mary's first glimpse of Canada when the *Aquitania* docked at Pier 21 in Halifax on September 19, 1949, was Halifax Harbour and Georges Island. After disembarking, her family members had to identify their luggage and pass through customs and the final stages of the immigration process, in the shed at Pier 21. Here they each received their Landed Immigrant cards and were free to begin their new life in Canada.

The family would not stay in Halifax, and had arranged with Canadian National Railways for travel to Toronto. CN acted as immigration agents, in co-operation with what was then known as the Departments of Colonization and Agriculture, a hangover from the days when immigrants were recruited to work on Prairie farms. The first thing Mary's family saw when they finally emerged from the immigration shed were the train tracks that linked Halifax with the rest of the country. Gathering their luggage, the family embarked on the train for the overnight journey to Montreal. From there they travelled to Toronto, where they were met by Mary's grown-up cousins and taken to her aunt's house.

Her father soon found work in Ajax, just east of Toronto, and the family settled down to make the adjustments all immigrants must when starting afresh in a strange place. There were some links with Mary's past life to ease her transition: her crate was unpacked and she was reunited with her doll carriage and dolls, toys, and books. She went to a new school, made new friends, grew up, and went to business college. After working for a few years, she got married, had children, and helped her husband run his business. Many years later, she brought her treasured doll carriage back to Halifax and donated it to the Canadian Museum of Immigration at Pier 21, where she told her story of a child's experience of leaving home and settling in a new country. This object truly has a tale to tell.

～44～

Schooner *Theresa E. Connor*

1938

Fisheries Museum of the Atlantic, Lunenburg

L UNENBURG HAS BEEN THE HOME PORT OF COUNTLESS FISHING
schooners. For over a century its legendary fleet formed the back-
bone of the region's economy. The most famous of the Lunenburg

schooners was of course *Bluenose*, built at the town's Smith and Rhuland shipyard. She was a working vessel, but also designed for speed. Between fishing voyages, her skipper, Captain Angus Walters, sailed her to victory in five international schooner races between 1921 and 1938. Fishing was her main business, but by the end of the 1930s the fishery was modernizing and the old wooden schooners were no longer considered commercially viable. After her distinguished racing career, *Bluenose* was sold to a West Indian company and was wrecked off Haiti while serving as a cargo vessel. Today she exists only as a replica, but the Fisheries Museum of the Atlantic still has one genuine representative of the wooden fishing vessels once so common along the Lunenburg waterfront: *Theresa E. Connor*.

Season after season throughout the nineteenth century, vessels left the harbour for the Grand Banks and the Labrador fishery and returned laden with cod. Building the schooners, manning them, and processing their catch provided employment for hundreds of people from the town of Lunenburg and neighbouring settlements. Spring and summer voyages were long, and in bad weather could be dangerous. The vessels were equipped with dories, from which the crew fished with baited trawls for cod, which they brought back to the mother ship.

Fishing from a dory on the open ocean was hard, sometimes hazardous, and often bone-chilling work. Once aboard the ship, the catch had to be gutted and cleaned, and salted down in the hold. Only then could the crew retire to the warmth of their quarters. Along the shore, the salt fish was air-dried on outdoor racks known as flakes, a process known as "making fish." (I have been told that in some places the flakes were covered on the Sabbath because "you don't make fish on a Sunday.") The dried fish was then packed in barrels for export, chiefly to the West Indies and southern Europe. For the domestic market, salt cod was packed in small wooden boxes.

Built in 1938 for the Halifax firm Maritime National Fish Company, and named after Theresa Eleanor Connor, whose family partially owned the company, it has been said that *Theresa E. Connor* was obsolete even then. It was the end of an era for the fishery's wooden schooners, which were being replaced by iron-hulled, engine-powered vessels. Nevertheless, she served well for nearly thirty years before becoming the first of a number of historic vessels to be moored at the Fisheries Museum wharf. Like *Bluenose*, she was built at Smith and Rhuland's Lunenburg shipyard. Unlike *Bluenose* and other schooners built in earlier days, however, she was equipped with a diesel engine as well as sails; she represents the transition from traditional sailing ships to power-driven fishing vessels. Maritime National operated her until 1952, when she was sold to Zwicker and Company Limited of Lunenburg.

Theresa E. Connor was one of the last sailing vessels to follow the traditional route—northeastward to the Grand Banks off southern Newfoundland—and being provided with an engine, she fished year-round, with shorter voyages in home waters in winter. She was equipped with twelve "double dories" and could carry a crew of twenty-eight men to the fishing grounds. Her hold could contain 425,000 pounds of fish. On the longer spring and summer voyages to the Grand Banks, the cod was packed in salt, but when fishing closer to home her crew used ice to preserve the fresh fish.

The schooner's first captain was Clarence Knickle, from Blue Rocks, near Lunenburg. He was succeeded by Captain Jack Mills, also from Lunenburg County. Her crew were mostly either from the neighbouring area or from Newfoundland. Her last captain was Harry Oxner, another local man, whose final voyage to the Banks took place in 1963, when modern trawlers had become the main working vessels of the fishery. Captain Oxner left Lunenburg that spring with a handful of men, intending to pick up most of his crew in Newfoundland before proceeding to the fishing grounds. When he arrived in Fortune Bay, he found it impossible to get a full complement of fishermen because most of them were already working on the trawlers—an easier life than fishing from dories. So Oxner spent the rest of the voyage with a reduced crew, fishing off Labrador with cod traps.

This episode marked the end of the salt bank fishery for Lunenburg schooners, and *Theresa E. Connor* spent the rest of her working life closer to home. In 1966 she was sold to the Lunenburg Marine Museum Society and served as a museum, a centennial project for the town of Lunenburg. When she was opened to the public in July 1967, her hold, once packed full of salted fish, housed the museum's exhibits of Lunenburg's maritime history, including charts, navigational instruments, sea chests, and other items donated by former fishermen's families. Today much of that original collection is displayed in the adjacent building, where the society now operates the Fisheries Museum of the Atlantic on behalf of the Nova Scotia Museum. Moored at the wharf close by, *Theresa E. Connor* remains open to the public, with displays reflecting the history of the salt bank fishery.

~ 45 ~

Halifax and South Western Railway conductor's hat

C. 1945

Halifax and South Western Railway Museum, Lunenburg

THERE WAS A TIME WHEN HATS LIKE THIS ONE WERE FAMILIAR sights on the South Shore, where trains wound their leisurely way along the line between Halifax and Yarmouth. These trains wandered by lakes and rivers and stopped at little stations along the way, picking up and dropping passengers and freight of all kinds. Heralded by the echoing sound of their steam whistles, they announced their arrival at stations and warned of their approach to crossings. For much of the twentieth century, they were an important component of rural life.

The initials CNR on this conductor's hat in the Halifax and South Western Railway Museum stand for Canadian National Railways, but the trains serving Nova Scotia's South Shore had not always been a part of CNR. In 1889 the first line in the area was the Nova Scotia Central Railway (NSCR), originally built to carry iron ore for export across the province. The route ran from Middleton to Lunenburg via Mahone Bay and through Bridgewater to serve business interests there, and was served by a mixed train consisting of a coach and some freight cars that ran daily except for Sundays. It was known as the "Blueberry Express," because it was said that it travelled so slowly passengers at the front of the coach could hop out and pick blueberries along the way, then catch the rear as it passed.

Efforts were made to link several more South Shore communities by rail, but with little success until the establishment of the Halifax and South Western Railway (H&SWR) Company in 1901. Serious work began in 1904, and in 1906 a line was opened from Halifax to Yarmouth, incorporating the already existing NSCR line between Bridgewater and Mahone Bay. Shortly afterwards, the H&SWR line was incorporated into the system operated by the Canadian Northern Railway Company, which in its turn became part of Canadian National Railways in 1918. The company operated a passenger service on the South Shore for just over half a century. Bridgewater, where locomotives took on coal and water, became the headquarters of CNR operations on the South Shore, complete with a roundhouse and an extensive shunting yard with several tracks where cars could be separated or assembled to make up trains.

Patrons of the Halifax and South Western, as it was still known, dubbed it the "Hellishly Slow and Wobbly": Nova Scotia has many hills and lakes, and in order to remain on relatively level ground with no steep inclines, the route had many kinks and curves, and the roadbed was not always smooth. The trains passed through some very scenic areas, but they ran slowly, and the refuelling along with the loading and unloading of freight took time. When diesel engines replaced the old locomotives around 1960, it was no longer necessary for trains to stop for coal and water, but as cars became more common and highways improved, people increasingly travelled and shipped goods by road. Passenger service on the H&SWR line was discontinued in 1969, though a dwindling freight service continued for another two decades.

This conductor's hat belonged to Charles Johansen, a long-time employee on the H&SWR line who lived in the Bridgewater area. He was born in northern Norway in an island lighthouse operated by his grandfather, where he spent many summers even after his family settled on the mainland. He went to sea in 1934 and joined the Norwegian navy at the outbreak of the Second World War, arriving in Canada the following year, after the fall of Norway. Johansen spent the first war years at Camp Norway in Lunenburg, where, as a chief petty officer, he trained other Norwegian sailors. The region must have impressed him, because after the war he decided to settle in Nova Scotia.

When Charlie left the navy in 1945, he found employment with the CNR on the Halifax and South Western line. He became a conductor, and was in charge of the train's overall operation and safety, as well as maintaining its schedule, overseeing loading and unloading of passengers and cargo, checking tickets, keeping records, and general responsibilities related to the train and its passengers. He worked out of Bridgewater, the hub of the railway's operations on the South Shore, where he married a local woman, settled, and raised a family in nearby Pleasantville. Charlie retained his love for the sea, and when he was not working on the railway he pursued a second career as a deep-sea fisherman, and for a while operated a charter business. When he retired, he had worked for the railway for thirty-four years, passenger service had been discontinued, and he was a conductor on a freight train. Charlie's last run on Train 517 was recorded in the local newspaper, and a crowd of friends and family gathered at the Bridgewater station to celebrate his retirement.

Charlie Johansen's hat is one of many memorabilia from the days of railway travel preserved in the Halifax and South Western Railway Museum. A model railway, representing the line around Bridgewater, is the centrepiece. Created in celebration of Bridgewater's centennial by an enthusiastic group of local volunteers, the model features Bridgewater

Station and its railway yards in a realistic panorama. Sadly the station itself no longer exists. Unlike several others on the line that have been preserved and repurposed, the abandoned Bridgewater Station building was mysteriously destroyed by fire in 1982. Its site, and that of the yards, was incorporated into a shopping mall, and a walking and cycling trail has replaced the tracks. But the old railway and those who worked on it are lovingly remembered in this museum.

~ 46 ~

Angus L. Macdonald's trowel

C. 1948

Chestico Museum, Port Hood

THIS HEART-SHAPED TROWEL SOMEWHAT RESEMBLES THE tool used by bricklayers and archaeologists in their everyday business. But they would never use a silver-plated, richly decorated implement like this for the serious work of spreading mortar or scraping away earth to reveal hidden artefacts. This particular trowel may have spread a token amount of mortar, but it was created for ceremonial purposes. The inscription on its surface tells its story:

> *This trowel was used for*
> *the laying of the corner*
> *stone of the*
> *Digby Rural High School*
> *by the*
> *Hon. Angus L. Macdonald*
> *Premier of*
> *Nova Scotia*
> *on*
> *June 17th 1948.*

So what is it doing in a small museum on the west coast of Cape Breton Island? Port Hood is a long way from Digby, and there seems to be little connection between them. But there are several similar trowels in the Chestico Museum collections, and the man who used them had close connections with the community. Among the souvenirs displayed in Port Hood's Chestico Museum, Angus L. Macdonald's silver trowels are tokens of his support of education in Nova Scotia.

Angus Lewis Macdonald, commonly referred to simply as Angus L., was born in Inverness County, Cape Breton, one of fourteen children. His family moved to Port Hood when he was fifteen years old, making their home in a former convent, the first in Port Hood. Young Angus attended the Port Hood Academy, and on graduation he taught in his hometown for two years in order to save money to attend St. Francis Xavier University. He continued to finance his studies by teaching and graduated with high marks, but his education was interrupted by the First World War. Just before the war ended, he was wounded while fighting with the Cape Breton Highlanders.

After a period of convalescence, Macdonald returned to Port Hood in 1919 and enrolled in Dalhousie's law school in Halifax that September. He graduated with distinction in 1921 and then worked for a short period in the Nova Scotia Attorney General's office before joining the law school faculty, where he became a popular professor. After taking a sabbatical year to earn a doctorate from Harvard, Macdonald returned to Dalhousie in 1929. The following year, he abandoned academic life in order to enter politics. He had been an active member of the Liberal party for some years and was now considering running for office.

With the support of his wife, Agnes, Angus L. Macdonald ran as the Liberal candidate in his home riding of Inverness in the federal election of 1930. (The museum houses a photo of him addressing the crowd from the balcony of the old Port Hood Court House, since burnt down.) Narrowly defeated, Angus L. returned to Halifax where he opened a private law practice, but he often visited Port Hood and maintained ties with the community. In October of that year, he attended the Liberal convention to elect a new leader. Neither of the two original contestants inspired much enthusiasm, and unexpectedly Angus L. was nominated from the floor. The delegates rallied around him, and he emerged after the first ballot as the leader of Nova Scotia's Liberal party. With no seat in the legislature, he had to lead his party from the public gallery, but he travelled widely, mustering support for the Liberals, and was seen as a latter-day Joe Howe, defending the rights of ordinary Nova Scotians against the elitist Tories. When a provincial election was called in 1933, the Liberal party achieved a landslide victory.

Angus L. was a popular and progressive premier of Nova Scotia from 1933 to 1940, including pre-war years that saw hard times in the province as a result of the Depression. He believed that people preferred the dignity of work to the humiliation of accepting relief. Until that time, there had been very few paved roads in the province, so his government created meaningful employment through major highway-improvement projects. Rural electrification was made a priority, along with promotion of the tourism industry. Angus L. also fought the federal government to obtain fairer treatment for poorer provinces, with funding for old-age pensions and unemployment insurance. Under his guidance, the Trade

Union Act gave workers the right to collective bargaining. He was no doubt influenced by the experience of growing up among hard-working people in rural Cape Breton.

Macdonald spent the war years in the federal cabinet as minister of defence in charge of the Canadian Navy. He built the service into an effective fighting force, fifty times larger than at the beginning of the war. In 1945 he returned to Nova Scotia and resumed his duties as premier, a title he'd hold until his death in 1954. While in office, he continued to work to gain more concessions from Ottawa for the province. His greatest postwar contribution to Nova Scotia was in the field of education. For the first time, a provincial minister of education was appointed; funding was provided to Dalhousie's faculties of law and medicine; the pattern of provincial education was modernized; and rural high schools were established, serving many students who previously had difficulty completing their education at small country schools.

All this leads us back to the trowel. The ceremonial laying of a cornerstone of a public building is a time-honoured practice, always carried out by a person of importance. When the institution is a school and the stone is laid by a politician, this gesture symbolizes the government's support for education in the region. The Digby Rural High School was established in 1948 to serve the young people of that area. The premier who had worked to implement its construction was an appropriate person to spread the symbolic portion of mortar for this stone, and this trowel is the implement he used. After the ceremony, the elegant trowel was presented to Macdonald as a souvenir, one of several he received on similar occasions and are now displayed in the Chestico Museum.

∼ 47 ∼

Whitney Pier mailbox

1960s

Whitney Pier Historical Society Museum

THIS VENERABLE CAST IRON MAILBOX SERVED THE POPULA-
tion of Whitney Pier for many years. "The Pier," as it is known
locally, lies on Sydney Harbour, Cape Breton Island, north of the
city centre, near Muggah Creek and the former site of the Sydney Steel

Plant. Although it has become a residential suburb of Sydney, Whitney Pier was once a separate community cut off, by the railway and the steel plant, from the rest of the town. It had its own small businesses, schools, cinemas, churches and halls, and a synagogue. Today, the former Adath Israel Synagogue houses the Whitney Pier Historical Museum. Its many treasures include this mailbox, which provided an important connection for The Pier's diverse immigrant society with the rest of the world.

Whitney Pier takes its name from Henry Melville Whitney. An American industrialist who came to Cape Breton and acquired most of its coal mines in the 1890s, Whitney was a member of the syndicate that established the Dominion Coal Company in 1893, and the Dominion Iron and Steel Company in 1899 (which, in 1928 would merge to form the Dominion Steel and Coal Corporation [DOSCO]). The "pier" at Sydney Harbour was the wharf built to load the coal brought by rail from Dominion Coal's nearby mines onto freighters. Workers were recruited for the loading operations, and when the steel plant began production there was work for many hundreds more.

The workers were mostly young men, who came from around the world to seek employment in the late nineteenth and early twentieth centuries. While Nova Scotia has been populated mainly by immigrants over the past four hundred years, most communities can trace their roots back to a particular part of Britain or New England. It is less common for a small community to have such ethnic diversity as can be found at Whitney Pier. Italians, Poles, Ukrainians, Croatians, Hungarians, Jews from all over Europe, Blacks from the West Indies, Chinese, Lebanese, Newfoundlanders, Scots, Irish, and others who had come to seek work in the mines or the steel plant all lived in its shadow, amidst the dirt and pollution common to heavy industries at that time. Workers were initially housed in crowded bunkhouses or boarding houses nearby, sometimes sleeping in shifts on shared bunks until they could afford homes of their own. After the First World War, many workers brought their wives and families to join them and bought, built, or rented houses. As the town grew, Jewish and Lebanese immigrants opened businesses in the area and the Chinese residents operated laundries and restaurants. Churches of various denominations served the community's many faiths.

There was a post office in Whitney Pier from the late nineteenth century, but this cast iron box bears the Canadian coat of arms adopted in 1921. In the 1960s boxes of this type, inscribed with *Canada Post Office*, replaced the Royal Mail boxes. The Whitney Pier mailbox was manufactured at the Sydney Steel Plant and remained in use for many years until Canada Post installed the bin-type boxes in use today. Most residents had left relatives behind in their home countries, and this mailbox was a vital link to the loved ones who waited eagerly for their news. The letters dropped into it would have told of the joys and sorrows, the expectations and disappointments that their writers experienced in their new home.

The community's fortunes were closely tied to those of the Sydney Steel Plant, which went through several changes of ownership during the hundred years of its existence. Its prosperity was subject to market fluctuations, and like many other industries the plant prospered during both world wars and suffered in times of recession. Periods of unemployment brought hardship to Whitney Pier, resulting, from time to time, in labour unrest. In 1967, under threat of closure by its owner, the plant was taken over by the provincial government. Despite these efforts, a century after it had opened, the Sydney Steel Plant closed its doors for the last time in 2000.

With the demise of the plant came a new challenge: its legacy to the area's disheartened residents was a desolate industrial wasteland due to the contaminated Coke Ovens site and the toxic sludge of the Tar Ponds, the residue of the Ovens' operation. There was general agreement that this mess needed to be cleaned up, but even after the Coke Ovens had been demolished, it was some years before environmental planners devised a way to dispose of the hazardous waste. Many meetings were held with local residents and a remediation plan was finally approved in 2007. The Sydney Tar Ponds Agency was appointed to oversee the plan's implementation, to be funded jointly by the federal and provincial governments. As a result, there was work again for the citizens of The Pier. Reclamation of the site took some years, but in 2013 the Tar Ponds cleanup was completed and a park opened on the former industrial site. Whitney Pier is now considered a clean, healthy residential area.

Throughout the community's history, the many ethnic groups in Whitney Pier found support from social networks centred on their churches, benevolent societies, and social clubs that preserved the traditions of their homelands. These traditions are featured in the exhibits of the Whitney Pier Museum and maintained by St. Nicholas Italian Roman Catholic Church, St. Philip's African Orthodox Church, Holy Ghost Ukrainian Catholic Church, and the Polish parishioners of St. Mary's Church, which, sadly, was destroyed by fire in December 2014. In recent times, closer integration between ethnic groups has taken place, but Whitney Pier maintains its diversity. Though once dismissed as a poor, working-class neighbourhood, The Pier has also produced a number of distinguished Nova Scotians, among them former Lieutenant-Governor of Nova Scotia Mayann Francis, Chief Justice J. Michael MacDonald, and former Speaker of the House of Assembly (2011–2013) Gordon Gosse.

When this mailbox was in use, mail was collected three times a day. Letters with a date stamp from the Whitney Pier post office were dispatched to distant places where residents maintained links with friends and family. Today, newer mailboxes have replaced the old, postmarks are less specific, and Whitney Pier is identified only by a Sydney postal code, but the community's continuing pride in its multi-ethnic identity is evident from the items in its museum.

～48～

Coldstream fly-tying bench

LATE 20TH CENTURY

Margaree Salmon Museum, Northeast Margaree

THIS PIECE OF FINE WOODWORK CAN BE FOUND IN A HIDDEN valley just off the Cabot Trail in Northeast Margaree. A former schoolhouse, the Margaree Salmon Museum is full of treasures celebrating the famous salmon-fishing river that flows near its door.

Both branches of the Margaree River, the Southwest and Northeast, are well known for salmon and trout fishing, and the Northeast Margaree particularly has attracted generations of sport salmon fishers from all over the world. The museum tells the history of the sport and introduces the life cycle of the salmon that spawn in the Margaree and return to it as adults. Visitors learn about the contribution of salmon and trout fishing to both the tourism and economy of the region, and are introduced to some of the people, famous and not so famous, who have taken part in and promoted the sport. Along with an aquarium displaying live salmon

and trout, there are also examples
of stuffed and mounted specimens
as well as numerous paintings and
photographs. Among the exhibits
is a collection of hand-tied flies—
many of which were donated by
their creators—used as lures. This
little fly-tying bench exemplifies a
craft that is essential to the sport.

Silver Doctor

The only legitimate way to catch a salmon in the Margaree is in-season,
with a rod, a line, and a permit. (As with any other game, poaching is
not unknown to happen—and the various types of spears used for this
purpose are also displayed in the museum—but this activity is not encouraged, and the museum emphasizes conservation.) Salmon can be lured
with a "fly" attached to a hook and floated on the surface of the water
by casting a light line with a long, flexible rod. The flies are artificial and
come in a wide variety of designs, often made by the anglers themselves.
Fly-fishing equipment has evolved over the years, and examples of rods,
reels, and lines from different periods form a large part of the exhibits.
Other gear on display includes rod cases, creels for the catch, and containers for flies. The flies themselves come in varying traditional shapes,
sizes, and colours and often have interesting names, like Silver Doctor
and Evening Star. The wide range of colourful creations on display in
the museum's cabinets speaks to the variety of colours, materials, and
designs that can be combined by a skilful fly-tyer.

But how are they made? Flies are tiny—many no more than a centi-
metre long, and some even smaller—and consist of a wide variety of
materials, both natural and man-made, making "fly-tying" a very skilled
and delicate operation. This small fly-tying bench made of bird's-eye
maple, for example, is not much bigger than a laptop. Still, while flies
can be purchased ready-made from suppliers of fishing tackle, many
experienced anglers prefer to make their own, following designs that
have proved to be successful in luring fish, or sometimes experimenting.

This fly-tying bench was the first of its type made by Derek Fraser of the Coldstream Fly Tying Furniture business. After surviving a fire in a fishing tackle shop in Dartmouth, it was donated to the museum by Derek Fraser of Stewiacke. As well as the working surface, on which flies are tied, the bench has rods to hold spools of silk and metallic thread, spaces for bottles of glue and varnish, and drawers for the fine, specialized tools used in tying. The bars at each side serve both as handles and as holders for tools and other materials. The spools on display show the variety of colours that might be used, combined with small pieces of wool, hair, fur, feathers, or whatever the design calls for. Once the materials have been selected, they are tied to make attractive lures that resemble various exotic and beautiful types of fly and then attached to a hook. It is exacting work that demands manual dexterity and good eyesight.

Recreational salmon and trout fishing have formed an important part of the Cape Breton economy for many years. Hotels and fishing lodges provide accommodation for anglers who visit from all over the world, expert guides are available for advice and instruction, and outfitters sell and rent fishing gear. The collection of artefacts and memorabilia in the Salmon Museum represents the panorama of people who have come from near and far to fish on the Margaree. Some are celebrities, but most are simply dedicated anglers whose gifts to the museum, like this little bench, provide insight into the history of the sport in Cape Breton.

～49～

Acadian hooked tapestry

C. 1980

Les Trois Pignons Cultural Centre, Chéticamp

THE MUSEUM OF THE HOOKED RUG AND HOME LIFE AT LES Trois Pignons Cultural Centre features the work of Chéticamp's rug hookers, particularly the well-known Elizabeth LeFort. But LeFort was by no means the only talented rug hooker of this region. Another imaginative wool artist was the lesser-known Catherine Poirier, who hooked this eye-catching hanging.

For the women of the Acadian villages on Cape Breton's northwest coast, hooking mats and rugs was originally the result of recycling worn-out clothing and old feed bags in order to furnish their houses. Their husbands were fishermen: money was short and the winters were long. Hooking was one of the ways in which these women, like others in rural Nova Scotia, occupied themselves and provided a little comfort and colour for homes that could not afford luxuries. Towards the end of the nineteenth century they also made finer, more decorative mats using wool from local sheep and plant dyes, which they sold to supplement the family income.

In 1927 their skills came to the attention of an American woman, Lillian Burke, who was visiting Chéticamp. Burke realized the commercial potential of the local craft and encouraged the Acadian women to perfect their hooking. She became their agent and marketed their work in the United States. The women now worked with new, dyed wool, hooking floral designs on fresh burlap, producing the fine mats for which Chéticamp has become well known. While individuals made small items, teams of women often made larger pieces while seated at a large frame on which the design had been traced. Some pieces were intended to enhance the floor and others to hang on the wall, where they were often known as tapestries.

Rug hooking became a successful local industry, and in 1963 the women of Chéticamp organized themselves into a co-operative. In this way they no longer depended on an agent who would sell their rugs and take a cut on the profits. They did their own marketing and set their own prices, providing a better return for their skilled work and bringing more prosperity to the community. While many women continued to produce the well-known floral mats of various sizes still popular among tourists today, there were also gifted individuals who developed their own personal style of pictorial imagery. While Elizabeth LeFort became famous for her realistic scenery and her portraits, Catherine Poirier developed a completely different, more imaginative approach when producing what she called her "sceneries."

Poirier's life spanned most of the twentieth century. Born in 1901 into a large family in St. Jospeh du Moine, near Chéticamp, she was taught the craft of hooking by her mother. She attended school until she was twelve, and then became absorbed into the life of the family, helping her mother in the house and tending the animals. Later, like many other Nova Scotians, Poirier left her community as a young woman to seek her fortune "down the road." In her case, the road led to Waltham, Massachusetts, where she lived for some years in the 1920s, working in a textile mill and then as a domestic servant. There were other people from Chéticamp in Waltham, and it was here that she met her husband, Moses Roach, whom she married in 1925. When the Depression brought hard times and unemployment to the United States, the couple returned home to stay.

In Chéticamp, rug hooking had become a valuable commercial skill since work was otherwise hard to find, and was the economic mainstay of the community. So Catherine Poirier started on a new career, in which she would find great success. Like most women of the area, Catherine began by working with the traditional designs for which there was a ready market. One of her rugs was awarded a prize in 1940, and she reproduced its pattern many times. But it was when she began to work on distinctive designs of her own in the 1970s that the popularity of her work grew. Catherine Poirier's tapestries depict scenes from daily life in Chéticamp in a primitive, playful style using bold colours, with strong representations of the houses, boats, people, and animals by which she was surrounded. After the years spent working in New England, Catherine returned to Chéticamp with a greater appreciation of her homeland. She loved its daily life: the card games, the singing, and the everyday activities. These became themes in her hooking, depicting village life as it was throughout much of the twentieth century. Her images included milking cows, hanging out washing, attending church, fishing, or bringing home the Christmas tree. Poirier's "sceneries" celebrated her community in a way that touched people's hearts, and this made her work very popular.

This tapestry depicting a winter scene in the village is typical of

Poirier's later work. Using bright colours, she juxtaposed an oversize red barn, houses of various sizes with smoking chimneys, a birdhouse the same size as a human house, and a variety of birds looking expectantly for food. Paths worn in the snow lead to the different buildings and a track leads over the hill. The sun hangs in a textured sky with multicoloured clouds. It is an affectionate portrait of a place she knew well.

Catherine Poirier's work attained more widespread recognition after some of her tapestries were displayed at the McCord Museum of Canadian History in Montreal in 1982. At the age of eighty-one, she attended the exhibition and was featured on radio and television, telling stories and singing songs that she had composed. In her later years, her sight failed and she was no longer able to do the fine hooking that had brought her fame. But she continued to enjoy the social life of the community, where she was a well-known personality. Catherine died in 1994, but her work lives on in tapestries such as this one.

～ 50 ～

Seven-headed beast
Mi-Carême mask

EARLY 21ST CENTURY

Le Centre de la Mi-Carême, Grand Étang

THIS MASK IS PART OF THE COLLECTION DISPLAYED AT LE Centre de la Mi-Carême (Mid-Lent Centre), at Grand Étang, part of the parish of St. Joseph du Moine in northeastern Cape Breton. While the masks on display in Grand Étang are recent, they represent an old tradition. This example, a seven-headed beast, depicts a version of a dragon-like monster from an Acadian folk tale that has been passed down in the Chéticamp region over many generations.

Masks and disguises are part of an ancient Acadian tradition that lives on in this region. The custom of celebrating Mi-Carême, or Mid-Lent, was brought from France to Acadie in the seventeenth or early eighteenth century. Until well into the twentieth century, the annual Lenten fast between Ash Wednesday and Easter Sunday was observed very strictly by the Catholic Acadian population. The faithful were called to six weeks of penitence and abstinence, but on the fourth Thursday of Lent the rules were relaxed. Austerity was forgotten, festivities returned to the community, and for that one day, fun and merrymaking prevailed. Music and dancing, card playing and dating, and a less restricted diet were permitted, reviving people's spirits before the fast was resumed for the remaining few weeks before Easter.

Until the mid-twentieth century, the traditional Mid-Lent festivities resembled today's Hallowe'en house-to-house expeditions or the visits of the mummers in Newfoundland. Young men of the village, masked and costumed and known as *les mi-carêmes*, travelled by wagon door to door around their village soliciting donations of food for the parish poor. At each household the residents were challenged to identify the disguised visitors, who were often invited in for music and dancing. If the items collected exceeded the needs of poor families, the surplus became a feast for *les mi-carêmes*.

Another traditional aspect of the Mid-Lent celebrations was the female character known as *La Mi-Carême*, a mythical figure who, like Santa Claus, brought treats for good children; on the other hand, those who had been bad would be carried away by her (children were known to hide under the bed or in a closet to avoid this fate). There were many variations of this tradition, including one in which *La Mi-Carême* took the place of the stork and delivered new babies. She was often portrayed as a terrifying witch-like creature, draped in a white sheet, wearing a black glove, and brandishing a stick. Unlike the visiting *mi-carêmes*, this sinister figure was often a family member in disguise.

As time went on, the Catholic church relaxed some of its former Lenten restrictions and the observation of the season became less onerous. The need for a day of respite was less urgent as a result, and in many Acadian communities the traditional Mi-Carême celebration was already dying out by the middle of the twentieth century. But it has survived or been revived in a few places, and it is still alive in the villages of Chéticamp and St. Joseph du Moine on the Cabot Trail. Here, it has developed from a brief period of relief from fasting to a week-long festival, with events in each of the neighbouring communities.

At one time, the arrival of *les mi-carêmes* on the doorstep was often the spark that initiated a full-blown kitchen party. Modern houses, unfortunately, are less suitable for spontaneous gatherings of merrymakers with muddy boots. While some homes still welcome *mi-carêmes*, today's festivities more often consist of social gatherings in community halls, and in Grand Étang, at this Mid-Lent Centre. Family members even travel great distances home to spend a few days enjoying the fun.

As at Hallowe'en, disguise has always been a central element of Mi-Carême festivities, but there have been changes over the years. The wearing of masks and costumes is no longer restricted to young men; today, women and children also participate. In former times, costumes were homemade, put together from discarded clothes and old bed sheets, and masks might be no more than a piece of cloth tied over the face, a layer of face paint, or a false nose. Today, used clothes may be kept on hand purposely for future disguises, costumes and accessories may be purchased and are often more elaborate, while masks are easily obtainable in stores.

In communities where the custom of Mid-Lent celebrations has survived, the mask remains an essential part of the disguise. Le Centre de la Mi-Carême was established in 1998 to encourage tourism by interpreting the Mi-Carême tradition. On display is a large collection of masks, including this one representing the seven-headed beast. Recounted in Père Anselme Chiasson's collection of Acadian folk tales, the story tells of a poor widow's son who saves a princess from being eaten by the seven-headed beast to whom a girl from the community is sacrificed each year. The girls are chosen by drawing numbers, and one year the king's daughter draws the fatal number. The tale has several twists and turns, but eventually the boy kills the beast and rescues the princess. The hero is, of course, rewarded by marrying the princess, his brothers marry her sisters, and the widowed king marries the boys' mother. The tale resembles traditional folk tales of dragons, but this mask makes the beast look more like a moose!

As part of the Centre de la Mi-Carême's interpretive experience, the tradition of making one's own disguise is reintroduced to visitors through mask-making workshops. The masks on display vary from grotesque to exotic and represent a wide range of imaginative creations. This seven-headed beast mask is hardly practical for an evening's wear, but it is an amusing interpretation of an old Acadian folk tale villain.

A Living Treasure:
Gus the Tortoise

BORN C. 1922

Nova Scotia Museum of Natural History, Halifax

A FTER THE FIFTY INANIMATE OBJECTS I'VE DESCRIBED, I'D like to close with something completely different: a living museum treasure. Gus the Tortoise has been a favourite among visitors to the Museum of Natural History in Halifax for many years and is one of the most appealing of its permanent exhibits. Gus, however, is not a native Nova Scotian. He is a gopher tortoise, born in Florida, and came here in 1942 with the then-director of the Nova Scotia Provincial Museum, Don Crowdis, who bought him for the princely sum of five dollars.

Gus's first home was in the Provincial Museum on Spring Garden Road, where he roamed freely and soon became popular among young and old. He was given the name Gus in honour of a young volunteer at the museum, John Augustus Gilhen, who would drop in to help after school and was particularly fond of the tortoise. Gus was about twenty years old when he came to Nova Scotia, and a relatively young animal. Now, he is thought to be the oldest living gopher tortoise in the world: the museum celebrated his ninetieth birthday with a party in the summer of 2012.

Tortoises and turtles are closely related reptiles, belonging to the genus *Testudo*. This Latin name was also used by the Romans to describe a defence method formed of interlocking shields, which *Testudo* shells resemble. The shell is tough, and it, too, serves a defensive purpose: a tortoise can withdraw its head and legs into it so that its body resembles a rock. This protective mechanism is useful for such a slow-moving creature, allowing it to easily take refuge from predators. The domed top of the shell is called the carapace, and the flatter underside is known as the plastron. And like their inhabitants, *Testudo* shells grow very slowly.

There are no native tortoises in Nova Scotia; however, there are four types of native turtle. Snapping turtles and painted turtles are quite common, while wood turtles are rarer and Blanding's turtles are limited to the protected habitat of Kejimkujik National Park. (These last two types are both considered at risk.) Marine turtles are sometimes seen in Nova Scotia waters, but are only summer visitors. Our turtles live in and around lakes and streams, and come ashore to lay their eggs at nesting time, in early to mid-summer.

As a gopher tortoise, Gus is adapted for desert conditions in the southern United States. Unfortunately, habitat loss due to development in that area has caused this species to be classed as threatened. But Gus lives safely in a sandy enclosed pen on the ground floor of the museum, with a lamp that provides warmth on chilly days. He is sometimes taken outside in summer to enjoy the sun and nibble on fresh grass and dandelion leaves. Like most of his species, he is a vegetarian and eats salad leaves and fruit. Since he is kept warm even in winter, Gus does not need to hibernate as many wild tortoises do, but he is less active in winter than he is in summertime.

My family first met Gus in the 1960s, when he lived in the Nova Scotia Provincial Museum's former quarters in the building on Spring Garden Road that now houses the Dalhousie School of Architecture. With the Halifax Memorial Library just across the street, a popular Saturday morning activity for many local children in those days was a visit to the library and then to the museum, where at that time admission was free. Staff and volunteers ensured that the youngsters had a good visit, and the highlight of the morning was Gus, who was usually out and about. There were also some long-suffering garter snakes that put up with being handled by a succession of children. Wary at first, the kids soon learned the proper way to make friends with them.

This was the beginning of a long association between museum-goers and Gus. Adults who have known him for as long as they can remember now take their own children and grandchildren to visit him in the museum's present quarters on Summer Street, now known as the Nova Scotia Museum of Natural History. When the collection was moved there in 1970, Gus went with the other exhibits and has been welcoming visitors ever since. He is not the only living exhibit; the museum is also home to turtles, salamanders, a variety of frogs, toads, and snakes, and a colony of bees. Sometimes it hosts visiting birds and animals, and in summer it maintains a butterfly house.

The museum keeps an increasingly urban population in touch with the natural world. Gus, although a "come from away," is a very special treasure who has introduced generations of children to his own particular branch of the animal kingdom, and to the natural history that is the essence of this museum. He has seen the provincial museum evolve from a miscellaneous collection of natural and historical objects in an old building to a modern facility interpreting the natural world. Gus has outlived many of his old friends, but remains a favourite with each new generation. Long may he continue to be a living treasure.

Epilogue

A S WE TRAVEL THROUGH NOVA SCOTIA ON BUSINESS OR ON vacation, often in a hurry and with our destination in mind, it is all too easy to pass by the blue key signs at the roadside that identify our many museums. We may make a mental note—*I should go and look at that sometime*—but somehow we never quite manage to get there.

I have shared with readers some of the treasures I have found in our museums, in what has proved to be a very rewarding project. These items have been preserved because they have stories to tell, not only about people and events that have shaped our history, but also about the daily lives of ordinary people in their kitchens and parlours, farms and fishing boats. The people who care for these items may be skilled professionals or dedicated volunteers, but they have all been generous in their willingness to take the time to guide me to what are, for them, significant items in their collections.

No doubt some readers have looked here in vain for their favourite object in their own favourite museum. To them, all I can say is that a book has physical limitations, and there are many objects I have enjoyed seeing and museums I have visited with pleasure, but which space has not allowed me to include. I have sometimes avoided describing a well-known item in favour of something that interested me and might otherwise be overlooked. I have tried to choose items representative of as many different aspects of our province's varied history and culture as possible, but I realize that there are many more stories to be told.

Nova Scotia has many wonderful museums, staffed by people who delight in introducing visitors to their treasures. Some are well funded, while others operate on a shoestring and represent a labour of love. Many community museums can open to the public only in summer, though the staff and volunteers may have been preparing material all winter for the coming season. So when you see the blue key sign on the highway as you travel around the province, take a little time to stop for a visit. And if there is a museum near you that you have always meant to investigate, or one that you have not visited for a long time, go and take a look. Maybe you will find your own treasure.

Acknowledgements

WHILE WORKING ON THIS PROJECT I VISITED MANY MUSEUMS, all of them filled with interesting objects. The items I have written about are my personal choices, but I frequently relied on knowledgeable museum staff to guide me through their collections, to introduce me to what they considered to be most interesting items and tell me their stories. Special thanks to the following people:

Donna Arenburg, Parkdale–Maplewood Community Museum
David Dewar, Wallace and Area Museum
Frank Dunn, Whitney Pier Historical Society Museum
Jocelyn Gillis, Antigonish Heritage Museum
Leah Griffiths, Shelburne County Museum
Frances Hart, Margaree Salmon Museum,
Nan Harvey, Colchester Historical Museum and Archives, Truro
Jennifer Hevenor, Canadian Museum of Immigration at Pier 21, Halifax
Sherry Hoffman and Teresa MacKenzie, McCulloch House Museum,
    Pictou
Frances Keddy, Ross Farm Museum
Margarete Kristiansen, Prescott House Museum, Starrs Point
Anne Marie Lane Jonah, Fortress of Louisbourg National Historic Site
Sunday Miller, Africville Museum, Halifax
Mary Pat Mombourquette, Cape Breton Miners Museum, Glace Bay
Moira Dianne O'Neill, Art Gallery of Nova Scotia, Halifax

Duane Porter, Halifax and South Western Railway Museum,
    Lunenburg
Linda Rafuse, Queens County Museum, Liverpool
Eileen Serroul and Jay Duguid, Jost House Museum, Sydney
Erika Smith, Nova Scotia Museum of Industry, Stellarton
Maynard Stevens and Bria Stokesbury, Kings County Museum,
    Kentville
Krystal Tanner, Alexandra Hernould, and Samuel Giles-Hogan,
    Randall House Museum, Wolfville
Susan Theriault, Uniacke Estate Museum, Mount Uniacke
Monika Viebahm, Haliburton House Museum, Windsor
Joanne Watts, Chestico Museum, Port Hood

And my thanks and apologies to those kind people who introduced me to interesting objects in their museums that I was unable to include in this book—not because they were unworthy of inclusion, but because space did not permit it. I would love to have been able to write about them all.

Thanks, too, to Patrick Murphy, managing editor of Nimbus Publishing, for encouraging me to pursue this project, and to editor Whitney Moran, for her careful reading of the text and valuable suggestions for its improvement.

Bibliography

M UCH OF THE INFORMATION IN THIS BOOK HAS BEEN derived from the museums in which these treasures are housed, and can be found in the museums' brochures and pamphlets, on their websites, and display panels. Above all, their curators have in many cases been generous in sharing their knowledge about items in their collections.

For biographical and historical information, I have made use throughout of the invaluable online version of *Dictionary of Canadian Biography*, to which many distinguished scholars have contributed, and of *The Canadian Encyclopedia*, also online. I have not cited individual references to these sources.

Background material has been provided by the following books:

Arsenault, Georges. *La Mi-Carême en Acadie*. Tracadie-Sheila, NB: Éditions La Grande Marée, 2007.

Bell, Winthrop P. *Register of the Foreign Protestants of Nova Scotia*, edited by Christopher Young. Vol 2. Guelph, ON: J. C. Young, 2003.

———. *The "Foreign Protestants" and the Settlement of Nova Scotia*. Sackville, NB: Mount Allison University, 1990.

Calder, John. *The Joggins Fossil Cliffs: Coal Age Galápagos*. Halifax: Nova Scotia Department of Natural Resources, 2012.

Chiasson, Anselme. *The Seven-Headed Beast and other Acadian Tales from Cape Breton Island.* Wreck Cove: Breton Books, 1996.

Clairmont, Donald H., and Dennis William Magill. *Africville: The Life and Death of a Canadian Black Community.* 3rd ed. Toronto: Canadian Scholars' Press, 1999.

Davis, Stephen A. *Mi'kmaq.* Halifax: Nimbus, 1997.

Denys, Nicolas. *Description and Natural History of the coasts of North America (Acadia),* trans. W. F. Ganong. Toronto: The Champlain Society, 1908.

DesBrisay, Mather Byles. *History of the County of Lunenburg,* 2nd ed. Toronto: William Briggs, 1895.

Dunn, Brenda. *A History of Port Royal/Annapolis Royal 1605–1800.* Halifax: Nimbus and The Historical Society of Annapolis Royal, 2004.

Eber, Dorothy Harley. *Catherine Poirier's Going Home Song.* Halifax: Nimbus, 1994.

Johnston, A. J. B, and W. P. Kerr. *Grand Pré: Heart of Acadie.* Halifax: Nimbus, 2004.

Lane Jonah, Anne Marie, and Chantal Véchambre. *French Taste in Atlantic Canada 1604–1758: A Gastronomic History.* Sydney, NS: Cape Breton University Press, 2012.

MacDonald, Carole. *Historic Glace Bay.* Halifax: Nimbus, 2009.

MacGregor, Neil. *A History of the World in 100 Objects.* London: Penguin, 2012.

Rand, Elizabeth. "The McKay Car." *Kings County Vignettes.* Kentville: Kings County Museum, 1989.

Roberston, Alexander. *Rules and Orders Formed for the Regulation of the Members of the Friendly Fire Club,* Shelburne 1784, ed. with notes by Mary Archibald. Halifax: Petheric Press, 1982.

Trask, Deborah. "The Edward Ross Diaries." *Journal of the Royal Nova Scotia Historical Society.* Vol. 9, 2006.

Whitehead, Ruth Holmes. *Micmac Quillwork; Micmac Indian Techniques of Porcupine Quill Decoration, 1600–1950.* Halifax: Nova Scotia Museum, 1982.

Whitelaw, Marjorie. *First Impressions: Early Printing in Nova Scotia.* Halifax: Nova Scotia Museum, 1987.

———. *The Dalhousie Journals.* Vol. 1. Ottawa: Oberon Press, 1978.

Whitney Pier Historical Society. *From The Pier, Dear!* Sydney, NS: Whitney Pier Historical Society, 1993.

Young, Christopher. *Maps Associated with Lunenburg Family History.* Guelph, ON: J. C. Young, 2003.

The following online material has also been valuable:

Hallett, Meghan P. "The Davison Family of Wallace and Pictou: A Case Study in Maritime Enterprise." Master's thesis, St. Mary's University, Halifax, 1998. http://www.collectionscanada.gc.ca/obj/ s4/f2/dsk2/tape17/PQDD_0002/MQ33844.pdf

Maclurg.com: "The McClurgs of Templemoyle." http://www.maclurg. com/Family/Templemoyle/Templemoyle.htm

Slaven, Sydney S. "The Birth of a Steel Mill—The Disco and Dosco Years." http://sydneysteelmuseum.com/history/birth_continued.htm

Young, J. Oscar. *History of the Ovens: A Story of the 1861 Gold Rush.* http://archive.org/stream/historyofovensst00younuoft/historyof- ovensst00younuoft_djvu.txt

Image Credits

Images by the author, with the following exceptions kindly provided by these institutions:

2 Mi'kmaw arrowhead: DesBrisay Museum Collection, Bridgewater, NS, photographer John Burnett, DB108.14

10 Saint-Ovide de Brouillon plate: Fortress of Louisbourg National Historic Site, Parks Canada/Heidi Moses/RAL-5359T

24 Scottish Presbyterian Communion token: Antigonish Heritage Museum, Antigonish, Nova Scotia

27 Portrait of Lieutenant Provo William Perry Wallis, by Robert Field: Art Gallery of Nova Scotia

32 Antique French wallpaper: Wolfville Historical Society, Randall House Museum, Wolfville, Nova Scotia

38 *Victorian* horseless carriage: Museum of Industry, Stellarton, Nova Scotia